King's Rhapsody

A Musical Romance

Ivor Novello

A Samuel French Acting Edition

SAMUELFRENCH-LONDON.CO.UK
SAMUELFRENCH.COM

Copyright © 1949 by Chappell & Co Ltd
Copyright © (Acting Edition) by 1955 by Samuel French Ltd
All Rights Reserved

KING'S RHAPSODY is fully protected under the copyright laws of the British Commonwealth, including Canada, the United States of America, and all other countries of the Copyright Union. All rights, including professional and amateur stage productions, recitation, lecturing, public reading, motion picture, radio broadcasting, television and the rights of translation into foreign languages are strictly reserved.

ISBN 978-0-573-08016-6

www.samuelfrench-london.co.uk

www.samuelfrench.com

FOR AMATEUR PRODUCTION ENQUIRIES

UNITED KINGDOM AND WORLD
EXCLUDING NORTH AMERICA
plays@SamuelFrench-London.co.uk
020 7255 4302/01

Each title is subject to availability from Samuel French,
depending upon country of performance.

CAUTION: Professional and amateur producers are hereby warned that *KING'S RHAPSODY* is subject to a licensing fee. Publication of this play does not imply availability for performance. Both amateurs and professionals considering a production are strongly advised to apply to the appropriate agent before starting rehearsals, advertising, or booking a theatre. A licensing fee must be paid whether the title is presented for charity or gain and whether or not admission is charged.

The professional rights in this play are controlled by Samuel French Ltd, 52 Fitzroy Street, London, W1T 5JR.

No one shall make any changes in this title for the purpose of production. No part of this book may be reproduced, stored in a retrieval system, or transmitted in any form, by any means, now known or yet to be invented, including mechanical, electronic, photocopying, recording, videotaping, or otherwise, without the prior written permission of the publisher. No one shall upload this title, or part of this title, to any social media websites.

The right of Ivor Novello to be identified as author of this work has been asserted by him in accordance with Section 77 of the Copyright, Designs and Patents Act 1988

KING'S RHAPSODY

Presented by Tom Arnold at The Palace Theatre, London, on the 15th September, 1949, with the following cast of characters—

(in the order of their appearance)

PRINCESS KIRSTEN } cousins of Princess Cristiane	Pamela Harrington
PRINCESS HULDA	Wendy Warren
MR TRONTZEN, the Dancing Master	John Palmer
COUNTESS VERA LEMAINKEN	Olive Gilbert
PRINCESS CRISTIANE	Vanessa Lee
KING PETER OF NORSELAND	Victor Boggetti
A MANSERVANT	Harry Fergusson
JULES, Nikki's valet	Michael Anthony
QUEEN ELENA OF MURANIA, the Queen Mother	Zena Dare
VANESCU, Prime Minister of Murania	Robert Andrews
NIKKI	Ivor Novello
MARTA KARILLOS, an actress	Phyllis Dare
COUNTESS OLGA VARSOV, a lady-in-waiting	Anne Pinder
FLUNKEY	Douglas Orr
MADAME KOSKA, a modiste	Jacqueline Le Geyt
MAJOR DOMO	Eric Sutherland
COUNT EGON STANIEFF	Denis Martin
VOLKOFF	Michael Anthony
1ST ROUGH	Michael Anthony
2ND ROUGH	John Palmer
3RD ROUGH	Larry Mandon
A TARTAR CHIEF } characters in the Muranian Rhapsody Ballet	Leon Biedrycki
A GEORGIAN GIRL	Trisha Colbourne
A GIPSY QUEEN	Joyce Hartwell
AN ALBANIAN BRIDAL COUPLE	{ Irene Claire / Ted Lane }
A MAID	Ann Carson
FOOTMAN	Douglas Orr
THE BOY KING	John Young
THE ARCHBISHOP	Michael Anthony

Chorus of

VILLAGERS, MURANIANS, MANNEQUINS, SERENADERS, GUESTS, OFFICERS, FLUNKEYS, SERVANTS, GIPSIES, TARTARS and DANCERS

SYNOPSIS OF SCENES

ACT I

SCENE 1 A room in the Summer Palace of the Royal Family of Norseland
SCENE 2 A sitting-room in a small hotel in Paris, in the year 1880. Morning
SCENE 3 Outside the Palace at Bledz, Murania
SCENE 4 A boudoir in the Palace at Bledz, Murania. Late afternoon
SCENE 5 The boudoir. A week later. Evening
SCENE 6 Outside the Palace, under the boudoir window
SCENE 7 The Ballroom of the Palace

ACT II

SCENE 1 The drawing-room of Marta's villa on the outskirts of Bledz. **Evening**
SCENE 2 The drawing-room of Marta's villa. Six months later. Late afternoon

ACT III

SCENE 1 The garden of the Summer Palace at Kalacz. A year later
SCENE 2 The garden of the Summer Palace. The same evening
SCENE 3 An anteroom in the Palace
SCENE 4 The Royal Box at the Paris Opera. **Ten** years later
SCENE 5 The Cathedral of Bledz, Murania

MUSIC PLOT

Overture

ACT I

1	The Dancing Lesson		Kirsten and Hulda
2	Chorus and Dance	"Birthday Greetings"	Chorus and Dancers
3	Song	"Some Day My Heart will Awake"	Cristiane
4	Reprise	"Some Day My Heart will Awake"	Cristiane
5	End of Scene Music		
6	Arrival at Murania	"The National Anthem of Murania"	Chorus
7	Song	"Fly Home, Little Heart"	Vera
8	Mannequin Parade		
8a	Exit Music		
9	Song	"Mountain Dove"	Cristiane
10	Song	"If This Were Love"	Cristiane
11	Quartet	"Mountain Dove"	Serenaders
12	Ballroom Scene		Chorus
13	Entrance of Marta		
14	Entrance of the King		
15	Entrance of Princess Cristiane		
16	Finale Act I Dance and Reprise	"Some Day My Heart Will Awake"	Cristiane
17	Entr'acte Music		

ACT II

18	Opening Dance		Dancers
18a	Exit Music		
19	Song	"The Mayor of Perpignan"	Marta and Chorus
20	Chorus	"The National Anthem of Murania"	Chorus
20a	Reprise	"The Mayor of Perpignan"	Marta and Chorus
21	End of Scene Music		
22	Trio	"The Gates of Paradise"	Cristiane, Vera and Egon
22a	Reprise	"The Gates of Paradise"	Vera
23	Entr'acte Music		

ACT III

24	Song and Ballet	"Take Your Girl"	Vera, Chorus and Dancers
24a	Melos		
25	Song	"The Violin Began to Play"	Cristiane
26	Ballet	"Muranian Rhapsody"	Chorus and Dancers
27	Reprise	"The Violin Began to Play"	Chorus
28	Opening Music, Scene 3		
29	Reprise	"Some Day My Heart Will Awake"	Orchestra
30	The Coronation Scene		Cristiane, Vera and Chorus

KING'S RHAPSODY

ACT I

SCENE 1

A room in the Summer Palace of the Royal Family of Norseland

It is a cool, elegant room with an air of complete informality. There are large french windows up C opening on to the grounds. A door down L gives access to other parts of the Palace and there is a staircase up L leading to further apartments. The french windows and a window in the R wall give a view of a fiord and distant snow-clad mountains. Below the staircase is a built-in seat. The furniture is of carved wood and light in colour. A large chest stands under the window R. There are two upright chairs, one RC and one L. There is a long low stool L. There is a clock on the wall of the staircase and decorative plates are used elsewhere on the walls and shelf of the stove.

When the CURTAIN *rises, sunshine streams in the windows and open doors up* C. PRINCESS KIRSTEN *and* PRINCESS HULDA, *cousins of Princess Cristiane, are having their dancing lesson under the Dancing Master,* MR TRONTZEN, *who stands down* L.

THE DANCING LESSON   No. 1

KIRSTEN *and* HULDA

At the end of the dance, KIRSTEN *and* HULDA *are breathless.* KIRSTEN *moves up* C. HULDA *sits on the stool* L.

HULDA. Oh, Mr Trontzen, was that better?
TRONTZEN. Better, yes—but not good. Now once again.
KIRSTEN. Oh, not again—I simply couldn't.
TRONTZEN [*crossing to* C] Now, Highness—if you want to please the Princess—after all, it's her birthday.
KIRSTEN. Yes, and she's having such a lovely birthday—ski-ing from dawn till now. I wish I was with her instead of this horrid dancing lesson. Oh, I'm sorry, Mr Trontzen, I didn't mean you were horrid.
TRONTZEN. Don't apologize, Your Highness—I hated my dancing lessons, too.
KIRSTEN. Oh, did you?—that has cheered me up. I wonder if I shall ever dance like you.
TRONTZEN [*crossing down* R] Not if you don't practise.

COUNTESS VERA LEMAINKEN *enters on the stairs.*

HULDA. But what's the use of practising?—we shall never perform publicly. That's the worst of being royal.

VERA *comes down the stairs.*

VERA. You must dance, because you love to dance—as I love to sing. [*She moves down* LC]
HULDA. Yes, but Countess Vera, you used to sing in public—for money, too.
VERA. I certainly did—and I'm not ashamed of it.
HULDA [*rising and crossing to Vera*] Was that when the King fell in love with you? [*She hugs Vera*]

KIRSTEN *giggles.*

VERA. Hulda! Really! [*She crosses to Trontzen*] Mr Trontzen—I hope you are not listening.
TRONTZEN [*moving the chair from RC down* R] I know when to be deaf, Countess. [*He glances at his watch*]
VERA. I see you are looking at your watch.
TRONTZEN [*with a step towards Vera*] My wife . . .
VERA. I know, your wife is expecting . . .

KIRSTEN [*moving to* L *of Vera*] Expecting what?

VERA. Expecting him for dinner, of course. You go, Mr Trontzen. I will attend to Her Highness—after all, she is two hours late.

TRONTZEN [*bowing and kissing Vera's hand*] Thank you, Countess Vera. [*He crosses to* LC, *turns and bows*] Good morning, Princess Kirsten, good morning, Princess Hulda.

TRONTZEN *exits down* L.

KIRSTEN. He's rather sweet. If I wasn't royal—I might consider marrying him.

VERA [*moving to the table*] But you are royal and he's got a very charming wife.

HULDA. Countess Vera, who *will* Cristiane marry?

VERA. The man of her choice.

KIRSTEN. But who? There aren't many eligible Princes left. Sweden and Denmark have grabbed them all.

HULDA [*crossing and sitting on the stool*] There's always the Balkans.

KIRSTEN. Oh, but they're so lascivious.

VERA. Kirsten! That is not a nice word.

KIRSTEN [*crossing down* R] I didn't mean it to be. [*She stops and turns*] What does it mean? Attractive?

VERA. It might—in certain cases.

KIRSTEN [*crossing slowly to the window* R] Like Nikki of Murania—was he attractive once? I mean, when there was all that scandal and he had to leave. [*She gazes out of the window*]

VERA. He chose to leave.

HULDA. But why, didn't he want to be king?

KIRSTEN. Oh, Hulda. [*She turns*] Don't pretend you don't know—he was in love with an actress. [*To Vera*] What was her name?

VERA. Marta Karillos.

KIRSTEN. Oh, yes—Marta Karillos. And she was a bad influence and was expelled from Murania—so he went too.

HULDA [*rising*] Does he hate being in exile?

VERA [*moving down* C] Why question me?—I never knew the man.

HULDA. Yes. [*She crosses to Vera and kisses her*] But you've lived such a long time and know everything.

KIRSTEN [*moving quickly to the window up* RC] Why doesn't Cristiane come—[*she gazes out of the window*] you don't suppose she's had an accident?

VERA. Don't say such things. [*She crosses down* LC] Of course she hasn't. She knows those mountains better than she knows her own heart.

HULDA. Perhaps she hasn't got a heart. Perhaps that's why they call her the Snow Princess—her heart was turned to ice.

VERA. That's a very pretty story but it doesn't apply to Cristiane.

Cheers and shouts are heard off up C.

That must *be* Cristiane.

PRINCESS CRISTIANE *enters up* C *from* L. *She is dressed in ski-ing costume of the period.*

KIRSTEN
HULDA } [*together*] Happy Birthday, Cristiane.

CRISTIANE. Thank you, Kirsten. Thank you, Hulda. And it is a happy birthday. [*She crosses to Vera*] Vera, I've never had such a lovely run—the snow was alive and I felt I was flying through space on a star. I always love my ski-ing but today it was the best ever—a kind of birthday present from God. [*She removes her cloak*]

VERA [*taking the cloak from Cristiane*] I don't want to hurry you, but you know the entire village is waiting to greet you, and these two have been practising a most difficult National Dance especially for you.

CRISTIANE. Couldn't I see them like this? Surely I needn't dress up—after all, we're not in the Capital.

VERA [*crossing to* RC] Well . . .
CRISTIANE. That's all right then.

KING PETER OF NORSELAND enters down L. *He carries a jeweller's case concealed behind his back.* HULDA, KIRSTEN *and* VERA *curtsy.* CRISTIANE *turns, sees Peter and crosses to him.* PETER *stretches out his arm and embraces her.*

PETER. God give you a happy birthday, my child.
CRISTIANE. He has, Father.
HULDA. Yes—but apart from God, what are you going to give her?
PETER [*moving up* C] Bless my soul, I'd quite forgotten.
KIRSTEN [*crossing up* R *of Peter*] He hasn't, his eyes are twinkling—and he's got something behind his back.

HULDA *moves above Peter and looks at the box in his hand behind his back.*

HULDA. It's a box, a black one, and it's got a French name and Rue de la Paix on it.
KIRSTEN. Oh, Hulda, you've spoilt it, he wanted it to be a complete surprise.
CRISTIANE. Well, so it is, I haven't heard a single word.
PETER [*crossing to* R *of Cristiane*] Oh, well, you must just as well have it for being so tactful, but a kiss first.

KIRSTEN *crosses to* R *of Hulda.*

CRISTIANE. And after. [*She kisses him*]

PETER *hands the jewel case to Cristiane.*

[*She opens the case*] Oh, Father. [*She moves down* RC]

KIRSTEN *and* HULDA *cross and stand either side of Cristiane.*

It's the most beautiful thing I have ever seen.
HULDA [*pulling Cristiane's left arm*] Oh, let me see.
KIRSTEN [*pulling Cristiane's right arm*] Oh, please, Cristiane.

The three girls admire the necklace. VERA *crosses to the stool* L *and puts the cloak on it.*

HULDA }
KIRSTEN } [*together*] Sapphires and diamonds.
PETER. My own design and carried out by Larouche of Paris.
CRISTIANE. Oh, Father, you darling. [*She crosses to Peter and kisses him*]
VERA. And am I not to have a look?
CRISTIANE [*crossing to Vera*] As though you hadn't seen it. [*She shows her the necklace*]
VERA. Never set eyes on it.
PETER. Vera, really!
VERA. Well, just a glimpse as it arrived.
PETER. And only just in time.
CRISTIANE. I shall wear it always, even in bed. [*She puts on the necklace*] Darling Father, why are you so sweet to me? [*She crosses and puts the case on the stool*]
PETER. I like you to have pretty things. Oh, by the way, my dear, I want a word with you, privately.
CRISTIANE. But of course.
VERA [*moving down* LC] Wouldn't it do when the village has made its birthday greeting—then they can all go to their midday meal.

KIRSTEN *moves up* R. HULDA *crosses to the stool.*

PETER. Are they waiting now?
VERA. Yes, and they have been waiting for nearly two hours. [*She picks up the cloak, moves to the door down* L, *opens it and beckons off*]
CRISTIANE. That's my fault. Couldn't they come in now?

PETER [*crossing to the stairs*] By all means, get it over. [*He stands on the stairs*]

A MANSERVANT *enters down* L. VERA *hands the cloak to him, then crosses and stands up* R.

[*To the Manservant*] Will you tell those who are waiting that Princess Cristiane will receive them now.

The MANSERVANT *exits down* L.

CRISTIANE [*moving behind the stool*] Shall we stand over here?
HULDA. Can we stand with you?
CRISTIANE. And get some of my presents—you shall not.

CHORUS AND DANCE

No. 2

" BIRTHDAY GREETINGS "

CHORUS *and* DANCERS

HULDA *crosses and stands with Vera.*

The CHORUS OF VILLAGERS *and* DANCERS *enter processionally up* C, *bearing gifts in parcels, dolls, small fir-tree boughs and bunches of flowers. They sing of their gifts as they bring them and present them to* CRISTIANE, *who has a smile for each. She places her presents on the stool.*

CHORUS.
Gracious lady, lovely lady
Here's a loyal salutation
For this royal celebration.
Friendship cheer you,
Love be near you.
Heaven send you
Happy meetings,
Joy attend you
With our greetings.
Night-time ease you
Daytime please you,
Blessing and caressing as you wake.
Queen of us all
We are very proud of this day,
We, one and all
Follow you for ever
Ever, yours for ever.
Bringing greetings
Birthday greetings.
Reddest roses, Easter lilies
Pretty posies, mountain gillies
Love bestowing, ever-flowing
May good fortune be thine
Gracious lady for aye
From this Festival day.

HULDA *and* KIRSTEN *do their dance and are joined by young* GIRLS *and* BOYS *who dance a National Dance.*

At the end of the Dance the CHORUS *and* DANCERS *exit.*

CRISTIANE [*crossing down* RC] Wasn't that enchanting? How they must have worked.
PETER [*coming down the stairs*] Yes, they are good souls.
KIRSTEN [*crossing and standing above the door down* L] Father Peter, we have been having an argument. Would you say that Cristiane had a warm heart? Countess Vera says she has.
CRISTIANE. That's because she loves me.

KIRSTEN. So do we, but we don't know you've got a warm heart.
CRISTIANE. I don't know myself—hearts are funny things.
HULDA [crossing and sitting on the seat L] You never flirt, you're famous for not flirting.
VERA [crossing and sitting on the stool] Hulda, you talk a lot of nonsense.
CRISTIANE. No, she doesn't. It's quite true—I don't flirt. I think it's a waste of time. [She draws the chair down R a little forward and sits]
KIRSTEN. Perhaps you've got a cold heart.
CRISTIANE. I don't know. It may be cold—it may be just asleep.

SONG   No. 3

"SOME DAY MY HEART WILL AWAKE"

CRISTIANE

[Over the music] But some day—some day . . . [She sings]
Some day my heart will awake
Some day the morning will break,
Music will open my eyes,
Showing the skies
Golden with rapture.
Maybe this gentle refrain
Some day will echo again,
Bringing my lover's caress
Bidding my heart say yes.

Lazy heart, lazy heart,
The leaves of summer fall and die.
But still you drift along the stream,
Not even troubled by a dream.
The birds are mating
But while you're waiting
Time slips by.

Some day my heart will awake
Some day the morning will break,
Music will open my eyes,
Showing the skies
Golden with rapture.
Maybe this gentle refrain
Some day will echo again,
Bringing my lover's caress
Bidding my heart say yes.

PETER. And now, you children, run away. [He crosses to C] I want to have a private talk with Cristiane.
KIRSTEN. Oh dear, we're always being sent away when anything interesting is being said.

HULDA rises and exits with KIRSTEN up the stairs. VERA rises and crosses to the stairs.

PETER. No, Vera, don't go away. You've always looked after Cristiane—I should like you to hear what I have to say.
CRISTIANE [rising and crossing to R of Peter] Am I to be scolded?
PETER. No, my dear, not scolded—frightened a little, perhaps.
CRISTIANE. Oh, no.
PETER [moving LC] Well, not exactly frightened.
CRISTIANE. I'm frightened now. [She crosses to R of Peter] Do please tell me what it is I've done.

PETER. You've done nothing, it's . . . [*He hesitates*]
CRISTIANE *looks at Vera.*

Cristiane, you know that some day you will—you must marry.
CRISTIANE. Oh yes, some day—[*she turns and crosses slowly and aimlessly to the window* R] but not for ages.
PETER. Sooner than that.
CRISTIANE. Oh, not too soon, besides I've met no-one I want to marry. [*She gazes out of the window*]
PETER [*wandering up* C] No, my dear, you haven't, but Princesses seldom do, these things are arranged. Of course, one always hopes.
CRISTIANE [*turning*] What does one hope, Father?
PETER. That the husband will—will be sufficiently . . .

VERA *moves to* R *of the stool.*

Oh, Vera, this is so difficult.
CRISTIANE. It isn't difficult, Father. What you are trying to tell me is that some day I must make a suitable marriage, I realize that. [*She moves down* R]
PETER. Cristiane—some day, is now.
CRISTIANE. Now?
PETER. Yes.
CRISTIANE. But . . .
PETER. Let me tell you in my own words. Our country has for some time been in negotiation with another country for a great increase in mutual trade.

CRISTIANE *turns away.* VERA *sits on the chair down* L.

[*He moves down* C] Murania has certain commodities which . . .
CRISTIANE [*turning*] Murania. Did you say Murania?
PETER. Yes.
CRISTIANE [*crossing to* RC] But the King of Murania is old and married—his son is exiled.
PETER. The King is dying and his son is to be recalled.
CRISTIANE. Recalled—but he has been away for twenty years—he gave up his rights.
PETER [*crossing to* L *of Cristiane*] He is ready and willing to return on one condition—*you*.
CRISTIANE. But he doesn't know me, he has never seen me.
PETER. No, that is quite true, he doesn't know you and he has never seen you, but he too must think of his country's welfare.
CRISTIANE. He didn't twenty years ago, he thought of himself and someone else.

VERA *slowly rises.*

PETER. That little affair, I am assured, is over and done with.
CRISTIANE. It can't be. He gave up his rights to the throne for her, how can it be over and done with?
PETER. It's twenty years, a long time, Cristiane.
CRISTIANE [*crossing to the chest*] It wouldn't be a long time for me if I loved anyone. [*She opens the chest and takes out a large scrap-book*] I want to show you something. [*She crosses to Peter and hands him the book*] Look.

PETER *opens the book and looks at it.*

PETER. This is most extraordinary. Vera, did you know about this?
VERA. I had an idea.
PETER. But it's full of him.
CRISTIANE. Yes, nothing but him. Every word that's ever been written about him, every photograph, every drawing, I've kept them all.
PETER. Then there's nothing more *I* can tell you except that the final decision will rest with you. [*He returns the book to Cristiane*] Your happiness comes first.
CRISTIANE. But you want it, you want it desperately, don't you?
PETER. Yes.

CRISTIANE. Then I want it, too—oh, not for your reasons but for my own. They've called me cold, and—and remote. Oh, I know—the Snow Princess. It hasn't always been kindly, that nickname, but all this is why, and now . . . [*She crosses to the chest and replaces the book on it*] Oh, Father, it's too good to be true.

PETER. Too good to be true—and I was looking forward to an hour of apologies for his character. There are still things you must know.

CRISTIANE. I don't want to know anything. [*She crosses to* R *of Peter*] Oh, Father, this isn't a dream, is it? I'm not going to wake up.

PETER. No, my dear, it's a reality, and a reality that has to be faced soon.

CRISTIANE. How soon?

PETER. As soon as the marriage contract is drawn up and you are ready.

CRISTIANE [*crossing below Peter to* LC] I shall be ready as soon as I am required to be ready. [*To Vera*] I shall have all my trousseau made here—that will give the village employment.

PETER. Well, upon my life—[*he crosses to* C] I've never seen a lady so willing.

CRISTIANE. Father—one thing I'd like to know. Has he asked personally for my hand?

PETER. No. All our correspondence has been with his mother, Queen Elena.

CRISTIANE. His mother! Well, she should know what he wants, and of course he cannot ask for himself—he's still in exile. [*She gazes at him for a moment*] Father, what's the matter?

VERA *moves up* LC.

You look suddenly different.

PETER. Do I? [*He turns away down* RC]

CRISTIANE [*crossing to* L *of Peter*] Yes. Tell me why.

PETER [*turning*] Oh, Cristiane, are you sure . . . This man—you've idealized him, haven't you?

CRISTIANE. In a way I have, but I've always felt he's been misunderstood, I shan't misunderstand him.

PETER. But supposing he's utterly selfish?

VERA. It's no good going on, Father Peter. Good girls always find bad men wonderful.

CRISTIANE [*crossing to* C] But why should you think he's bad?

The MANSERVANT *enters down* L.

MANSERVANT. Your Majesty, Mr Wainikin has arrived and requests an audience, and *Mrs* Wainikin would be glad if Countess Vera would receive her.

VERA. Oh well, if I must.

PETER *crosses to the chest, picks up the scrap-book and looks through it.*

CRISTIANE. Oh, Vera, please not here. I don't think I could quite stand Mrs Wainikin just at this moment.

VERA [*to the Manservant*] I'll see her in my own room, Valdo, ask her to wait.

The MANSERVANT *exits down* L. CRISTIANE *crosses to Peter.*

PETER. Now, Cristiane—Wainikin is waiting to know. Arrangements will have to be made immediately—there are certain conditions we shall have to insist on. There will be many tiresome documents for you to sign—you'll hate all that. [*He places the book on the chest*]

CRISTIANE. I shan't even read them, I think I can trust you, Father. Can't I, Vera?

VERA. As much as you can trust any man. Are you coming, Father Peter? [*She curtsies*]

CRISTIANE *curtsies and moves down* R.

PETER. Yes, yes, I'm coming.

REPRISE

No. 4

" SOME DAY MY HEART WILL AWAKE "

CRISTIANE

VERA *exits down* L.
PETER *gives Cristiane a searching look, crosses and exits down* L.
CRISTIANE, *deep in thought, picks up the scrap book and turns the pages.*

CRISTIANE. Foolish heart, foolish heart
Your lonely hours have almost gone.
The morning hills begin to burn
And winter's tide is on the turn.
[*She moves down* C]
If clouds are flying
And winter dying
Why sleep on?

The RUNNING TABS *close behind Cristiane*

Some day my heart will awake
Some day the morning will break,
Music will open my eyes,
Showing the skies
Golden with rapture.
Maybe this gentle refrain
Some day will echo again,
Bringing my lover's caress
Bidding my heart say yes.

LIGHTING CUE 1

At the end of the song the lights dim quickly to BLACK-OUT.
During the BLACK-OUT, CRISTIANE *exits.*

SCENE 2

A sitting-room in a small hotel in Paris, in the year 1880. Morning

There are double doors up C *leading to the entrance hall, and a door down* R *leading to Nikki's bedroom. A window* L *overlooks the street. There is a small table, covered with a plush cloth,* LC *with two upright mahogany chairs, one above it and one* R *of it. An armchair stands by the window and there are upright mahogany chairs down* R *and down* L.

When the RUNNING TABS *open, the window curtains are closed and the light is dim. The stage is empty. Almost immediately the double doors up* C *are opened and* QUEEN ELENA OF MURANIA, *the Queen Mother, sweeps in. She is followed on by* VANESCU, *the Prime Minister of Murania, and by* JULES, *Nikki's valet.* VANESCU *carries a dispatch-case.*

JULES [*crossing to the window*] Would you take a chair, Madame? [*He opens the window curtains*]

LIGHTING CUE 2

The lights come up.

ELENA [*moving down* C] Be good enough to announce our arrival to Monsieur . . . What name does he go by here?

VANESCU *moves down* LC.

JULES [*crossing to* RC] Monsieur Dubois.
ELENA. How very original—why not Durand?
JULES. That, Madame, was in Nice.
ELENA. And in London?
JULES. Robinson. I fear, Madame, M'sieu Dubois is still asleep.
ELENA. Then wake him.
JULES. He would discharge me.
ELENA. You will be discharged in any case—so you have nothing to lose.
JULES. I might lose my position, Madame—but I do not wish to lose my life. M'sieu is apt to be violent if woken from sleep.
ELENA [*sitting* R *of the table* LC] Vanescu, deal with this man.
VANESCU. What does M'sieu Dubois pay you?
JULES. I have quite forgotten, it is so long since we spoke of money matters. No, M'sieu, I cannot be bought—M'sieu Dubois is my hobby, one does not sell one's hobbies.

ELENA. He may be your hobby—but he is also my son.
JULES [*recognizing her*] Your Majesty. [*He kneels*]
ELENA. Get up at once—I am here strictly incognito.
JULES [*rising*] May I look through the keyhole?
ELENA. Is that your usual custom?
JULES. No, Madame, but sometimes in the morning, M'sieu is not alone.
ELENA [*rising*] Then I shall look through the keyhole. [*She crosses to the door down* R *and peers through the keyhole*] You are quite safe, M'sieu is alone. [*She crosses to* C]
JULES [*crossing to the door down* R] Then if you will permit me . . .

JULES takes a key from his pocket, softly opens the door and exits down R.

ELENA. Locked in. The key on the outside. You know what that means.
VANESCU. He seems devoted.
ELENA. My son has always inspired devotion in the wrong people. I hope he wasn't too drunk last night, people can be obstinate after too much to drink. Will you tell him or shall I?
VANESCU. Officially I should be the one, as Prime Minister.
ELENA. Is the Prime Minister of Murania of more importance than the Queen?
VANESCU. The Queen Mother.
ELENA. Oh yes, I keep forgetting. No, I have decided, I shall tell him.

JULES *enters down* R.

JULES. M'sieu will be with you immediately, Madame. He is even now putting on his dressing-gown. He is—alas, unshaved.
ELENA. That does not surprise me. You may go.

JULES *exits down* R.

You have the list of eligibles?
VANESCU. In my dispatch-case.
ELENA. Give it to me.

VANESCU *takes a document from his dispatch-case*.

JULES *enters down* R *and stands to one side*.

JULES [*announcing*] M'sieu Dubois.

NIKKI *enters down* R. *He is in a dishevelled state and wears a dressing-gown and slippers.* ELENA *crosses to Nikki and sinks into a deep curtsy.*

JULES *exits down* R.

NIKKI [*raising her*] Oh, Mother, stop play-acting, and give me a kiss.

ELENA *kisses Nikki*.

[*He rubs his chin*] Sorry about the beard.
ELENA. But you realize the significance of my curtsy?
NIKKI [*crossing down* C] You always overdid everything, Mother. Greetings, M'sieu Vanescu. By the way, why are you in Paris in August? Why didn't you let me know you were coming?
ELENA. There was no time, it was all so sudden. Dreadfully sudden.
NIKKI. What was sudden?
ELENA. Vanescu, kneel to your monarch.

VANESCU *kneels*.

NIKKI. Kneel? [*He crosses to* L *of Elena*] Monarch? Good God, is the old swine dead? [*He turns and crosses to Vanescu*]
ELENA. I will not hear your father called old.
NIKKI [*raising Vanescu*] When did this happen?
ELENA. Two days ago.
NIKKI. There has been nothing in the papers.

ELENA. No, it is not official. It will not be official till you are back in Murania.
NIKKI. Oh, no, Mother. I've tasted freedom for twenty years, and I'm not going back.
ELENA. Not even on your own terms?
NIKKI. With you alive? No, Mother. If I went back, I say *if*, I should want it *all* my own way.
ELENA. And you shall have it. Oh, Nikki, aren't you tired of squalor? Just look at this room.

JULES *enters down* R. *He brings on a small table set with coffee for three, which he places up* RC.

NIKKI. Look, Mother, don't let's try to deceive each other. If my delightful cousin Cyril were to seize the throne, you'd be nowhere—an exile—wandering over Europe with only your memories, but with me, you'd still be Queen Mother and you want that. It's as simple as that.

JULES *exits up* C.

ELENA [*sitting above the table* LC] No, Nikki, there's more than that. I can't *bear* seeing the end of our Dynasty.
NIKKI [*crossing to* RC] Dynasty? It's just a word.
ELENA. It's a word that goes back eight hundred years—unbroken.
NIKKI [*crossing and sitting* R *of the table* LC] Well, it's broken now.
ELENA. It needn't be. Oh, Nikki, don't let Murania go to Cyril. He paid us a state visit last year, he was quite unbearable. His look of ownership, don't you agree, Vanescu?
VANESCU. I do indeed, Ma'am. [*He sits on the chair down* L] He's ready to move in and will, directly the news of your father's death is known.
NIKKI. The country—would they let him in?
VANESCU. Some would—less than half—and then civil war—bloodshed.
ELENA. Oh, Nikki, think of our little country torn in two.
NIKKI. And how do I stand? I mean, with the people.
ELENA. My darling boy, you're an idol.
NIKKI. Since when?
ELENA. Oh, for some time now—we've seen to that. We've played up the romantic story. " He gave up the throne for love."
NIKKI. But he didn't. [*He rises*] He gave up the throne for hate. Hate, Mama. [*He moves to the coffee table*] Oh, yes, I made no secret of the reforms—that's where I went wrong—I should have waited—[*he pours three cups of coffee*] plotted—said one thing when I meant another—and then that glorious day—my coming of age—when I faced my father and asked for a separate household. One glance from those implacable steely eyes and I knew—I just wasn't going to count at all. A highly paid servant of his will—not a move was I to make without his knowledge and consent—my friends banished, my own personal liberty curtailed. [*He picks up two cups of coffee, moves down* C *and hands one of them to Elena*] That six months of discipline in Old Fortress—I shan't easily forget that—it finally broke me. To hell with the good of the people—I'd learnt to hate. Coffee, Mama? [*He crosses to Vanescu and hands him the other cup of coffee*]
ELENA. Thank you. You're talking a lot of melodramatic nonsense—you gave up your rights for an infatuation.
NIKKI [*crossing to the coffee table*] An infatuation that lasted twenty years—not that I knew it would, then. [*He picks up a cup of coffee for himself*] Oh no—Marta was my excuse—a very charming one but only an excuse. [*He moves down* RC]
ELENA. Well, you might have chosen worse—she had a great charm. By the way, how is Marta?
NIKKI. Extremely well.
ELENA. Does she still do her little operettas?
NIKKI. She does indeed. She's doing one now.
ELENA. I must go and see her. I forgot, I can't, I'm in mourning. [*She sips her coffee*] So you still see each other?
NIKKI. You mean are we still lovers?
ELENA. Nikki!
NIKKI. Oh yes; we're still lovers.
ELENA. Faithful?
NIKKI. After twenty years? Darling, do grow up.

Scene 2 KING'S RHAPSODY 11

ELENA. Oh, I am so relieved. Vanescu, have you that list?   MUSIC
VANESCU [*rising*] I have it here. [*He crosses to* L *of the table* LC, *puts his cup on it, then lays the document on the table in front of Elena*] May I suggest . . .?
ELENA. No, you may not. [*She puts down her cup*]
NIKKI [*crossing to* R *of Elena*] Why are you so relieved?
ELENA. About Marta and you. Your marriage . . .
NIKKI [*choking*] My what?
ELENA. Your marriage. We can't have a bachelor on the throne. [*She rises*] We must have an heir.
NIKKI. Mother, you go too fast. [*He moves up* R] I've decided nothing.
ELENA. I rather think you have. Now, Nikki, this marriage.
NIKKI. I won't discuss it—at least not now. If I come back, I want time to look round.
ELENA. There is no time to look round. Marta, of course, must be given her congé.
NIKKI [*putting his cup on the coffee table*] Never.
ELENA. Oh, darling, only officially. This girl you're going to marry, she's only a figurehead—the heir provider. You shall have your Marta. I don't want to deny you anything. Only Nikki, you must decide.
NIKKI. I must say, there's only one thing about the whole proposition that attracts me—I should like a son.
ELENA. Very well, then.
NIKKI. I would have preferred him not to be a Crown Prince, but probably to me he'd be just a son. Someone I could bring up as I wasn't brought up. [*He crosses to* R *of Elena*] And, Mother, any interference from you with him and I shall have you killed.
ELENA. Ah, that's my boy talking.
NIKKI. By the way, did my father die a natural death?
ELENA. But, of course. [*She sits above the table* LC] My own doctor looked after him. Oh, Nikki, he was getting more and more difficult.
NIKKI [*sitting* R *of the table* LC] And so you thought of me.
ELENA. You were never out of my thoughts.
NIKKI. But supposing Marta and-I were married?
ELENA. You're not!
NIKKI. No, we're not. I wanted it and so did she, but we both agreed that a live Marta was better than a dead one. Your agents are so thorough, darling, aren't they?
ELENA. I adore efficiency. Oh, by the way, I shall settle a million on your son.
NIKKI. Not on me? Oh, darling, you must. After all, you can't take it with you.
ELENA. But I'm not going. Besides, you might slip away again.
NIKKI. No—not again. I want a second chance—I didn't think I'd get it. My father said he'd live for ever and I believed him. But he didn't—he's dead and now the job's mine. Can I do it? Perhaps it's too late—perhaps not—we'll see.
ELENA. That's settled then. We shall travel overland tonight.
NIKKI. Tonight?
ELENA. Of course. Vanescu, tell him what you arranged.
VANESCU. We shall be in Bledz by Thursday morning—the death will be announced after you have spent the night at his bedside praying for his recovery. You will be proclaimed, and twelve hours later your engagement will be announced.
NIKKI. You've forgotten one little detail—who is the lucky girl?

            VANESCU *crosses and sits down* L.

ELENA. Let me see now . . . [*She picks up the document*] Oh, there's the list. [*She studies the document*] Adela of Saze Wertzburg—they turned you down—so did three others, aren't they fussy? Here we are—marked with a cross—Cristiane of Norseland.
NIKKI. Cristiane of Norseland, never heard of her.
ELENA. No, darling, you wouldn't have. They lead a very quiet life—very rich, sapphire mines, coal, silver and forestry. Oh, it's a wonderful match.
NIKKI. Does she know about me?
ELENA. I don't think so or she wouldn't have said yes.

B

NIKKI. She said yes! Mother, you work too fast.   MUSIC
ELENA. I have to, I know my own son.
NIKKI. But do you know who his father was?
ELENA. Well, I'm a bit vague about that.
                              VANESCU *rises and moves to the window.*
Nikki, you're disgraceful!
NIKKI. And so are you, you—[*he fondles Elena's hand*] always were and you always will be.
ELENA. Oh, do you think so? That has cheered me up. Vanescu, I hope you're not listening.
                              JULES *enters up* C.
JULES. Sir, a lady has called and wishes to speak to you.
NIKKI [*rising*] Don't be diplomatic. You mean Madame Karillos has called.
ELENA. Nikki, send her away.
NIKKI. I've never sent her away yet. Show Madame Karillos up.
                              JULES *exits up* C. ELENA *rises.*
No, Mother, you've got to face her.
ELENA. I was always very fond of Marta. [*She crosses down* R] She always kept you out of mischief.
At least, I always knew where I could find you. Will you tell her or shall I?
NIKKI. I'll do that.
                              JULES *enters up* C.
JULES [*announcing*] Madame Karillos.
                      MARTA KARILLOS *enters up* C. *She is in her early forties but still
                      very attractive. She does not at first notice Elena and Vanescu.*
MARTA [*as she enters*] Good morning, Jules. [*She crosses to Nikki*] Nikki, you're not even dressed
and we lunch at one.
                              JULES *exits up* C.
NIKKI. Marta. [*He indicates Elena, then moves up* C]
MARTA [*startled*] Your Majesty! [*She sinks into a deep curtsy*]
ELENA [*crossing to* R *of Marta*] Marta, how charming to see you—[*she raises Marta*] and you look
so well. That gown! Worth?
MARTA. Yes, Ma'am.
ELENA. I thought so. Do you know the Prime Minister? Madame Marta Karillos.
VANESCU [*moving down* LC *and bowing*] Enchanted, Madame.
ELENA. I was passing through Paris on my way to Berlin, I couldn't resist a sight of Nikki. Now,
Nikki, I have endless fittings. Vanescu, have you the envelope with the instructions about tonight?
                              MARTA *crosses above Elena and stands down* R.
VANESCU [*taking some documents from his case*] Yes, Ma'am. I have it here.
ELENA [*indicating the table* LC] Leave it there—yes, on the table.
                              VANESCU *puts the documents on the table* LC.
Au revoir, Marta. I hope we shall be seeing more of each other in the future than we have in the past.
[*She moves to Nikki*] Good-bye, dearest boy, don't worry about anything. I've arranged it all per-
fectly. [*She moves to the doors up* C] Come, Vanescu.
                              MARTA *makes a deep curtsy.*
                              ELENA *exits up* C. VANESCU *crosses and follows her off.*
MARTA. And what did that visitation mean?
NIKKI [*moving down* C] The King is dead. The news has been suppressed to give me time to get there.
MARTA. You're going back?
NIKKI. Yes.
MARTA. Funny, I've seen this moment for twenty years, sometimes clearly, sometimes dimly, but
it's always been there. [*She crosses slowly down* LC] Why aren't I crying? Making a scene? I should
be . . . [*She stands with her back to Nikki*]

NIKKI [*crossing to* R *of her*] No.
MARTA. Oh yes, I should be. Why not?
NIKKI [*turning her to face him*] Because it's going to make no difference.
MARTA. No difference?
NIKKI. Not to us. This time I shall have absolute power, absolute freedom.
MARTA. Freedom for a King? A King! Oh, I forgot, I must curtsy. [*She curtsies but instead of rising, stays down, puts her hands to her face and weeps*]

NIKKI *raises her*

And whom will you have to marry?
NIKKI. Isn't it awful—[*he paces up* C *and turns*] I don't even remember. Cristiane of somewhere, I know, Cristiane of Norseland.
MARTA. Cristiane of Norseland? Oh yes, I remember her—[*she moves to* R *of the table* LC] her father succeeded last year. I don't envy her. You're an uncomfortable family.
NIKKI [*moving to* R *of her*] You'll help me, won't you? I shall need you.
MARTA. No, you won't, but I'll be there if you ever do. [*She touches his cheek*] Oh, darling, you do need a shave. [*She sits* R *of the table* LC] Your Snow Princess will make you shave twice a day.
NIKKI. Snow Princess! Why do you call her that?
MARTA. That's what they do call her in the cheaper papers. The Snow Princess! Oh, my poor Nikki.

NIKKI *moves above the table* LC *and looks at the documents.*

NIKKI [*presently*] Will you look at that. Pretty thorough, dear Mama. [*He calls*] Jules! Jules!

JULES *enters up* C.

JULES. Yes, sir.
NIKKI [*indicating the documents*] Read these carefully—make all arrangements. We're leaving Paris tonight.
JULES. For the South, M'sieu?
NIKKI. For Murania, Jules. For Murania.
JULES. Yes, Your Majesty—may I proceed with the arrangements?
NIKKI [*handing the documents to Jules*] You may.

JULES *collects the coffee table and exits with it up* C.

Dear Jules—did you notice his manner?—he's already forgotten the times he's poured me into bed unconscious—he thinks everything's changed. [*He crosses down* R]
MARTA. Everything has changed.
NIKKI. Nothing has. I'm going home to do a job—I hope to do it well. My private life will be my own. Do you remember the Villa Flora—on the Hervat Road?
MARTA [*rising*] Remember it!
NIKKI [*sitting on the chair down* R] That shall be yours—not too near the Palace—not too far away.
MARTA. Do your plans really include me?
NIKKI. If they did not, there would be no plans.
MARTA [*crossing to* L *of Nikki*] Oh, Nikki, promise me you'll never be loyal to me. I don't think I could bear it—just take me for granted.
NIKKI. I'm afraid I always have—have you minded?
MARTA. Have I seemed to?
NIKKI. If you had I shouldn't have known.
MARTA. Nikki, I want you to. Give the whole thing a little thought, Nikki. Go back—see how things are and then send for me. Oh, don't worry, I shall come.
NIKKI [*rising*] I shall send a regiment to fetch you.
MARTA. You'll need your regiments at home—a telegram will do.
NIKKI. I've already sent it.

14　　　　　　　　　　KING'S RHAPSODY　　　　　　　　　ACT I

MARTA.　Darling—they've been good these years. Ups and downs, but on the whole—good.　　MUSIC
NIKKI.　Yes—on the whole, good.

END OF SCENE MUSIC　　　　　　　　　　　　　　　No. 5

LIGHTING CUE 3

The lights dim quickly to BLACK-OUT *as—*

the RUNNING TABS *close*

SCENE 3

Outside the Palace at Bledz, Murania

The scene is a frontcloth with entrances R *and* L.

When the RUNNING TABS *open an enthusiastic crowd of* MURANIANS *are awaiting the arrival of Cristiane. Cheers are heard and the National Anthem of Murania is fervently sung.*

ARRIVAL AT MURANIA　　　　　　　　　　　　　　No. 6

"THE NATIONAL ANTHEM OF MURANIA"

CHORUS

CHORUS.　　Dear land of Song
　　　　　　And Liberty
　　　　　　We hymn thy ancient name.
　　　　　　Thy songs are strong
　　　　　　And true to thee,
　　　　　　The champions of thy fame.
　　　　　　From age to age
　　　　　　Thy heritage
　　　　　　Shall proudly dwell secure
　　　　　　On heath and hill
　　　　　　Thy spirit still,
　　　　　　Undaunted, shall endure.

LIGHTING CUE 4

At the end of the Anthem, the Lights dim quickly to BLACK-OUT *as—*

the RUNNING TABS *close*

SCENE 4

A Boudoir in the Palace at Bledz, Murania. Late afternoon

The boudoir has been prepared as Cristiane's private sitting-room. It is of very Baroque architecture and vivid colouring. There are double doors leading to a corridor up LC, *an ornate fireplace* L *and french windows* R *leading to a balcony overlooking a courtyard. There is an ornate baby-grand piano and stool up* RC, *and a tall cabinet* L *of the double doors. A settee stands* LC. *A small circular table with armchairs above and below it, stands in the window. There is an oval table below the piano, with an armchair* R *of it. Another armchair stands down* L. *There are exotic flowers on the piano.*

When the RUNNING TABS *open, the windows are open and outside can be heard the sound of bells and the shouts and cheers of the populace.* ELENA *is standing near the window, listening.* COUNTESS OLGA VARSOV, *a lady-in-waiting, is standing in the open window, gazing out.*

ELENA. Very satisfactory—they'll cheer themselves hoarse, get very drunk and go to their homes and by the time they have slept it off—we may have some news of the King. Olga, he's a madman. One gesture. That was all that was needed—one appearance on the balcony holding her hand—but no, he must rush away and hunt. Are there not three hundred and sixty days in the year for his hunting? This country is riddled with wild animals. Of course, it was done deliberately—a studied insult. What am I to say to her?

OLGA. Well, Ma'am, you could say that the yacht arrived a day earlier.

ELENA. But it didn't—it arrived a day later—yachts always do. She's with him, of course—this is her doing. [*She moves to the piano and studies the bowls of flowers on it*] Oh, why didn't I get rid of her in Paris?—it would have been so easy. And it was all going so smoothly. [*She picks up one of the bowls of flowers*] The King was quite acquiescent until those fatal papers arrived from Norseland demanding that Karillos should be sent out of the country—[*she crosses to the cabinet up* L] as if an innocent girl would even know of her existence. [*She decides against putting the bowl on the cabinet*]

OLGA. Oh, Ma'am, the whole world knows of her existence.

ELENA [*crossing to* C] Even all the way up there in Norseland. These diplomatists. We only pay them to keep these things quiet. What's going to happen when she knows that Karillos is here? Within a stone's throw of the Palace—and being constantly visited. [*She replaces the bowl on the piano*] She'll go home before the wedding and then what's to become of us all? There's no other available Princess —and why should there be?

OLGA. Ma'am—you must try and compose yourself—the Princess has entered the Palace.

ELENA. I must pull myself together, find excuses—he's ill—urgent business in the country. What does she look like?

OLGA. I couldn't see, Ma'am.

ELENA [*picking up the bowl of flowers*] Then shut the window.

OLGA *closes the window and crosses to* R *of the piano. The sound of cheering fades.*

I can't think with all that noise. I wonder what this girl is like. I wonder what I was like when I first came to Murania? They are the same cheers—the same flags by the look of them. [*She hands the bowl to Olga*]

A FLUNKEY *enters and stands to one side.* OLGA *puts the bowl on the piano.*

FLUNKEY [*announcing*] Your Majesty—Her Highness Princess Cristiane.

CRISTIANE *enters. She is followed on by* VERA. CRISTIANE *wears a charming costume and looks very nervous.*

ELENA. My dear child, welcome—welcome to Murania. You're exquisite, my dear, what a bit of luck.

CRISTIANE *curtsies.*

[*She raises Cristiane and kisses her on both cheeks*] I expect you are very weary from your journey.

CRISTIANE. A little, Ma'am. May I present my dear friend and lifelong companion, Countess Vera Lemainken.

ELENA. You are very welcome to Murania, Countess.

VERA [*with a curtsy*] Your Majesty.

ELENA [*indicating Olga*] Oh, this is Countess Varsov. She will I'm sure be most helpful to you. Sit down, my dear child, and you too, Countess—we are quite informal when we are by ourselves. [*She crosses and sits on the settee at the left end*]

CRISTIANE *sits* R *of Elena on the settee.* VERA *crosses above the settee to the armchair down* L *and sits.*

Now tell me, are you pleased with your reception?

CRISTIANE. But overwhelmed—I hadn't expected such affection.

ELENA. Our people are so easily moved—almost too demonstrative at times. I expect you will find them quite a change.

CRISTIANE. In what way, Madame?

ELENA. Well, South and North.

CRISTIANE. I have never known anything but affection from my people. Surely the human heart is the same over the world.
ELENA. I hope you will find it so. Do you like your little room?
CRISTIANE [*looking around*] It's enchanting.
VERA. Charming.
ELENA. Thank you. This is your own. Have you any hobbies?
CRISTIANE. Hobbies, Ma'am? I sing a little. The Countess does too—very beautifully.
ELENA. Good—you see your piano, and I have placed some of our National music on it. It might amuse you to study it.
CRISTIANE. It will give great pleasure, Ma'am.
ELENA [*rising*] Now tonight.

VERA *rises.*

[*She crosses to* C] I have arranged nothing for you—I knew you'd be tired. You would like to dine quietly up here and perhaps an early night—tomorrow you will, of course, show yourself in public. We will drive through the town together. And we must talk about clothes—I see you go in for simplicity—that is good—but it must be the right kind of simplicity.
CRISTIANE. I have quite an elaborate trousseau. Our people were very generous, they embroider very beautifully.
ELENA. Embroidery! Does that still go on? I must inspect it all tomorrow. I expect your maids are already unpacking—you would like to retire early I'm sure.
CRISTIANE. Retire, Ma'am? Before my meeting with the King?
ELENA. The King. But he's dead. Oh, Nikki—how stupid of me—of course, Nikki. I cannot tell you how excited he has been, he has made himself quite ill. [*To Vera*] Oh, would you mind sitting down, Countess?

VERA *resumes her seat.*

Oh, he has such a nervous temperament and then this unfortunate trouble in the Eastern Province. He actually had to go himself to quieten things down. He's so beloved. I said to him, " Nikki—[*she picks up the bowl of flowers and takes them down* R] go yourself even if you're not back for Cristiane's arrival. I will explain everything to her." And after all, what is a day or two, you've all your life together. [*She looks at the bowl*] What am I doing with this? [*She crosses to Olga*] Take it, Olga, and never let me see it again. [*She hands the bowl to Olga. To Cristiane*] Oh yes, so you see, my dear, he had to go. You know what the personal touch means.
CRISTIANE. But, Ma'am . . . [*She rises*]
ELENA. Oh, I know you're disappointed, it's only natural you should be, but when you see him it will all be forgotten. I shall leave you now—I am sending you a typical Muranian dinner—very light, of course, but I think you will enjoy it. [*To Vera*] Au revoir, Countess . . . ?
VERA [*rising*] Lemainken.
ELENA. Countess Lemainken, I must practise that.

ELENA *exits and is followed off by* OLGA.

CRISTIANE. She's very beautiful, isn't she?
VERA [*crossing to the piano*] As hard as nails.
CRISTIANE. She was lying, wasn't she, about—about Nikki?
VERA. Of course, there *has been* unrest in the Eastern Province.
CRISTIANE [*crossing to* C] Enough to take him away from the Capital the day his bride arrives? And yet, perhaps, it's just as well. I'm looking so tired, he'd hate that.
VERA. We're all tired and very nervous.
CRISTIANE [*indicating the portrait on the cabinet*] Oh look, there's his portrait. [*She crosses to the cabinet and studies the picture*] He's older than I imagined—his mouth smiles but his eyes don't smile. [*She turns*] Oh, Vera, let's go home now—tell them. It's not too late, say I'm ill, that I've changed my mind. Look, the Royal Yacht is still in the harbour. Oh, Vera, I'm afraid—[*she crosses to Vera*] take me home where they love me—take me home. [*She bursts into tears and throws herself into Vera's arms*]

VERA. There, there, my sweet, cry if you must—but it's going to be all right. [*She leads Cristiane to the settee.*
CRISTIANE *sits on the settee.*
You must believe me. Do you remember when you were very little those headaches you had—you always came to me and I used to sing you to sleep.
CRISTIANE. Yes, I remember—but it's all so long ago.

SONG

No. 7

"FLY HOME, LITTLE HEART"

VERA

[*Over the music*] In another world.
VERA. No, no, it's just the same—you're still my little girl, and I can still charm your tears away.

As VERA *sings,* CRISTIANE *grows gradually calmer.*

LIGHTING CUE 5

During the song the lights commence to fade.

VERA. Far, far away where the clouds hover low
I heard a cry like a bird in the snow,
Soft was my answer, " Have comfort, my dear,
Why waste a moment when April is here? "

Fly home, little heart,
Although the way be long,
Your wings are brave and strong
Fly home where you belong.
We know, little heart
How lonely you must be
So far across the sea,
So fly, little heart, fly home to me.
[*She moves down* C]

Fly home, little heart,
Although the way be long,
Your wings are brave and strong
Fly home where you belong.
We know, little heart,
How lonely you must be
So far across the sea,
So fly, little heart, fly home to me.
Fly home, dear heart, fly home to me.

The RUNNING TABS *close behind Vera.*

Soon as the dusk brings the end of the day
Wistful and sweet rings that song far away.
Out of the silence a voice thro' the foam
Yearning for love and the old times at home.

Fly home, little heart,
Although the way be long,
Your wings are brave and strong
Fly home where you belong.

We know, little heart,
How lonely you must be
So far across the sea,
So fly, little heart, fly home to me.
Fly home, dear heart, fly home to me.

During the BLACK-OUT, VERA *exits.*

SCENE 5

The boudoir. A week later. Evening

When the RUNNING TABS *open* CRISTIANE *is seated on the settee, watching a fashion parade.* MADAME KOSKA, *the Modiste, is standing down* R. CRISTIANE *is wearing a peasant costume. Five* MANNEQUINS *parade during the music, displaying négligée and gowns.*

MANNEQUIN PARADE   No. 8

At the end of the music the MANNEQUINS *are posed around the room.*

KOSKA. Does my poor collection please Your Highness?
CRISTIANE. Please me! They're perfectly lovely.
KOSKA. Then which may I select for you?
CRISTIANE. All.
KOSKA. All?
CRISTIANE. I want them all.
KOSKA [*crossing to* C] Your Highness is too gracious. [*She moves above the settee*]
CRISTIANE. Not at all. My poor embroidered trousseau—made so lovingly—how ridiculous it looks before all this—I wonder why I troubled to bring it. Take everything to my bedroom—I shall wear a different dress every day.

EXIT MUSIC   No 8a

The MANNEQUINS *exit up* LC.

KOSKA. Your Highness—may I be impertinent and make a very personal request? That little dress you are wearing, it is quite delightful.
CRISTIANE. This? But this is what our peasants wear.
KOSKA. But the shape and that line—it has real chic.
CRISTIANE. Thank you.
KOSKA. I assure Your Highness that it could set a fashion. After all, anything Your Highness wears, everyone will want to wear. Could I presume?
CRISTIANE. You mean you would like to copy it?
KOSKA. If you would do me so much honour.

VERA *enters up* LC *and crosses to* C. *She wears peasant costume.*

CRISTIANE. Vera—Madame Koska wants to copy my little peasant dress—wouldn't Astrid be thrilled?
KOSKA. Astrid? Another dressmaker?
CRISTIANE. No—just a little peasant girl—she made this for me.
KOSKA. And yours, too, Countess, could be adapted for the fuller figure. [*She gestures with her hands*]
VERA. I wear it for comfort. [*She crosses to the fireplace*]
CRISTIANE [*rising*] I shall have it sent to you tomorrow. [*She crosses to* C]
KOSKA. A thousand thanks, Your Highness. Oh, may I express my deepest sympathy with you over the King's illness.
CRISTIANE. Oh, he's much better—I may be allowed to see him tomorrow.
VERA [*anxiously*] I think perhaps Madame Koska would like permission to leave, Princess.
CRISTIANE. Of course—how thoughtless of me. Good-bye, Madame. [*She moves down* RC] I shall not forget the dress.
KOSKA. Your Highness, a thousand thanks for all your graciousness. You are going to look so adorable at the Court Ball. How I wish I could be there. [*She moves to the doors*]

CRISTIANE. Would you really like that?
KOSKA [*turning*] Your Highness!
CRISTIANE. I shall personally send you an invitation.
KOSKA [*overwhelmed*] Your Highness!

MUSIC

                      KOSKA *curtsies and exits up* LC.

CRISTIANE. Did I do that well? About the King, I mean.
VERA. Very well. But it was most impertinent of her to ask.
CRISTIANE. But why? Everyone in Bledz is enquiring—after all, it's a week. A whole week. Oh, Vera, it's almost funny—what if he never comes at all—what if we never meet? The Royal Romance that ended in smoke.
VERA. Smoke! [*She crosses to* C] If he doesn't come soon it will end in a bomb.
CRISTIANE [*moving to the window*] I know. It frightens me. They're living on a volcano—and for some strange reason, I'm stopping it erupting. Why is he humiliating me like this? I've never done him any harm—I only said "yes". Perhaps that's why he hates me so much, that he cannot face me. [*She sits in the chair below the table* R]
VERA. Cristiane, there's another reason. They've been trying to keep it from you. Marta Karillos is here in Murania. He's with her now.
CRISTIANE. So that's the reason for it all—I'm beaten before I start.
VERA [*crossing to Cristiane*] My dearest child—you must decide—are you staying?
CRISTIANE. I don't know—I don't know.
VERA [*moving to the window*] A message to your father and he would send a fleet to bring you back.
CRISTIANE [*rising and crossing to the piano*] He's with her now—he never wanted me—except to be of use.
VERA. Royal engagements have come to nothing before now. Everyone will blame him—not you, never you.
CRISTIANE. Does it matter who they blame? [*She turns to face Vera*] Leave me now, my dear. Tomorrow morning I'll give you my decision—[*she crosses below the settee to the fireplace*] but one thing I know, I've got to think it out alone. Good night.

                    VERA *crosses in silence to the door.*

VERA. Oh, I so hate having to tell you—but you were bound to know some time and it might have been too late.
CRISTIANE. Perhaps it's too late now.
VERA. Too late now.
CRISTIANE. Good night, Vera. Don't disturb my maids, I can manage for myself—I think I shall enjoy it.

                    VERA *shakes her head and exits.* CRISTIANE *wanders miserably about the room, notices the portrait on the cabinet, crosses to it and is about to throw it on the ground, then changes her mind and looks at it.*

Now I know why your eyes don't smile—poor trapped Nikki.

SONG

"MOUNTAIN DOVE"

CRISTIANE

No. 9

                    CRISTIANE *replaces the photograph, wanders to the piano, picks up a piece of music and idly starts humming. She then sits at the piano and plays and sings the song, a folk song of Murania.*

                      NIKKI *enters during the song. He wears riding clothes and a cloak. He carries a fur hat. He is slightly drunk.* CRISTIANE *does not at first notice him.*

CRISTIANE.   Farewell, my little Mountain Dove
                    The winds are calling you away.
                    I too can feel their stern command
                    That none may disobey.

>   Your last, lamenting serenade
>   Has lulled the summertime to sleep.
>   New loves await your roving song
>   And I am left to weep.
>   Ah, no! But quickly come
>   And lighten with your song the burden of my love;
>   For now there is nothing but farewell,
>   My little Mountain Dove.

MUSIC

NIKKI [*standing by the door*] That was charming.
CRISTIANE [*looking up*] Oh, you startled me.
NIKKI. Forgive me.
CRISTIANE [*rising*] Who are you?
NIKKI. An audience of one—clamouring for more.
CRISTIANE. I know who you are.
NIKKI. Why? Have the new stamps come out? But they're only profile. They always say my face is two profiles stuck together. [*He lurches to the piano*]

> CRISTIANE *backs away.*

So this is my bride's apartment, is it not? And are you my bride or has she retired to bed like a virtuous young lady—and if she's retired to bed why are you playing the piano?

> CRISTIANE *realizes Nikki is slightly drunk and that he has not realized who she is.*

CRISTIANE. Oh, she lets me play the piano—that is, when she's not here.
NIKKI. Oh, she does! By the way, aren't you being a little disrespectful? You should be calling me " Your Majesty ". But don't if it disturbs you—after all, we are both off duty. [*He sits in the chair below the piano*] Where is my bride?
CRISTIANE. If Your Majesty had been here for the last week, Your Majesty would know that Her Royal Highness is at the Opera, where she should have been accompanied by Your Majesty . . .
NIKKI. That's enough Majesty to last the whole night. So she's at the Opera, is she, and you've got to wait up until she comes in. The Opera, as I remember, finishes at midnight—that gives us two hours of each other's company—here, let me look at you. You're quite pretty. How wrong people are. I was informed that she was fat and getting on in years—you are the friend and companion, I gather?
CRISTIANE. Not even that—Countess Vera Lemainken would hardly wear a peasant's dress.
NIKKI. If she looks like you she would—it's good that dress, it shows off the scenery. I've made you blush—I didn't think they could blush north of the Danube. I should like some wine—I know I've had enough—but I want too much. Get me some.
CRISTIANE [*crossing below Nikki*] I can send for a footman.
NIKKI [*catching her by the hand*] And spoil our *tête-à-tête.*
CRISTIANE. There's some wine in the cupboard.
NIKKI [*releasing her*] Then get it, my dear child, get it. [*He rises and crosses to the settee*] I shall make myself comfortable.

> CRISTIANE *crosses to the cabinet up* L *and opens it.*

CRISTIANE. There's one bottle, but it's very dirty. [*She takes the bottle from the cabinet*]
NIKKI. And what's it called?
CRISTIANE [*reading the label*] Tokay—Imperial Tokay.
NIKKI. Tokay! And you've never tasted it?
CRISTIANE. I've never heard of it.
NIKKI. What an experience for you. Tokay for the first time. Is there a corkscrew?
CRISTIANE [*looking in the cabinet*] There is.
NIKKI. Then give it to me.

> CRISTIANE *takes the bottle and corkscrew to Nikki.*

Glasses! Bring two—now.

> CRISTIANE *goes to the cabinet and gets two glasses, which she takes to Nikki.*

It has to be opened very delicately. Not one of the original cobwebs must be disturbed—and they're all dated. [*He opens the bottle*]

CRISTIANE *holds the glasses while* NIKKI *fills them*.

CRISTIANE. It's a pretty colour.
NIKKI. Wait till you taste it. [*He takes a glass from her*]
CRISTIANE [*sipping her drink*] But it's quite nice.
NIKKI. Quite nice? Thank your stars that the peasants who bottled this can't hear you—you'd be lynched. Quite nice! [*He puts the bottle on the floor and drinks*] Go on—try it.

CRISTIANE *takes a long drink*.

Oh, not so fast, it should be sipped. Look—like this. [*He sips*] A bottle of Tokay would last a peasant family a year.
CRISTIANE. And we shall finish it in ten minutes.
NIKKI. But the effect will last for ever. Oh, it's good, it's good—dangerous, too—I haven't eaten since breakfast.
CRISTIANE [*sinking on to the settee*] Oh, it's doing funny things to me.
NIKKI. Already? Try some more—or are you afraid?
CRISTIANE. I'm afraid of nothing. [*She picks up the bottle and refills her glass*]
NIKKI [*holding out his glass*] And one for me.
CRISTIANE. But should you be drinking? You've had a fever.
NIKKI. A fever?
CRISTIANE [*refilling his glass*] Of course. At least that's what we were told—that you were quite ill. You must have been, otherwise you would have been here to greet us. [*She puts the bottle on the floor*]
NIKKI. Was that the story? Well, it's as good as any other. [*He sits* L *of Cristiane on the settee*] But I'm not going to lie to you—there's something about you that I like—I wonder what it is? I know what it is, you're Northern—nothing dark and deep and devious about you. I'm going to tell you something, but you must keep it to yourself. I wasn't ill at all, I had no fever—I stayed away deliberately and I'd have stopped away—sent her back to the frozen North—but I discovered something—I like being King and they like me.
CRISTIANE. You mean, if you had sent us back, they might not have liked you so much?
NIKKI. How right you are. This marriage is apparently my salvation—I'm a reformed character—my God, if they only knew. This girl means nothing and never will—I'm prepared to accept her, I need an heir—she could have given me one—now she's not going to have the chance.
CRISTIANE. But why? Why this hatred? You don't even know her.
NIKKI. Perhaps not, but I know her signature on a shameful arrogant scrap of paper. " If Madame Marta Karillos is forthwith expelled from Murania." That was the phrase she used. Good God! Doesn't she realize this is purely a marriage of convenience? How dare she dictate to me, how shall I behave to the only utterly loyal person I ever knew. " Expelled from Murania." [*He rises and faces the fireplace*] That was the phrase that drove me mad—her one unalterable condition.
CRISTIANE. And this condition was signed by her?
NIKKI. In triplicate.
CRISTIANE. She might not have realized.
NIKKI. Impossible.
CRISTIANE [*rising*] No, not impossible.
NIKKI. What do you know of such things? [*He finishes his wine and slowly turns*]
CRISTIANE [*picking up the bottle*] Nothing, but I've been with her so long, I know her as well as I know myself. [*She moves* C]
NIKKI. This is very interesting—you can tell me some details about her. [*He crosses to* L *of her*] What's your name?
CRISTIANE. Astrid.
NIKKI. Astrid. Give me some more wine, Astrid. It's a charming name.

SONG

"IF THIS WERE LOVE"

CRISTIANE

The music of the Serenaders is heard outside the window and continues under the dialogue.

[*He puts his glass on the table* C *and crosses to the window*] Good God—my serenaders. You see, I was going to do the whole thing properly—Serenaders under her window.

CRISTIANE *puts her glass and bottle on the table* C.

My mother will love that—so will the Press. Listen to them—swooning violins—the National love songs—the whole filthy bag of tricks.
CRISTIANE [*crossing to* RC] Do you love Marta Karillos?
NIKKI [*turning*] What did you say?
CRISTIANE. Do you love Marta Karillos?
NIKKI. With all my heart and soul.
CRISTIANE. And body?
NIKKI. You mean, am I faithful to her? Yes, when I remember.
CRISTIANE. Well, if you are not all the time, what can it matter?
NIKKI. What indeed! You are very direct. Very well, I shall be direct, too. Oh no, the Princess and I shall marry—why not? We are expected to—we shall go our own ways. [*He crosses to the settee*]
CRISTIANE. And the heir?
NIKKI. The heir? Oh, he must be an unrealized hope for the moment. [*He sits on the settee*] Well, you're one of her loyal servants, why don't you slap my face or are you afraid of being killed?
CRISTIANE. I wasn't even listening, I was only hearing the music.

LIGHTING CUE 6

The lights dim a little.

NIKKI. Take no notice—it's only a cheap, effective trick. It's tricking me now—I'm finding you attractive.

CRISTIANE *hums the music, crosses and kneels below the settee.*

You're humming my favourite song. Sing it to me.
CRISTIANE.
    If this were love,
    Deep tender love,
    This hour were an hour divine.
    If all this were true
    Gentle and true
    Then earth and heaven would be mine.
    The sky would burn with a million stars
    And moonlight dance along the sea,
    If this were love and I were in your arms
    And you were in love with me.

The music continues. NIKKI *listens, quite fascinated. As* CRISTIANE *finishes the song he catches hold of her arms, and she makes no attempt to get away.*

NIKKI. If this were love—perhaps it is—one kind of love. You know, you're very sweet. [*He holds her hands*] Are you as cold as your countrywoman—what's she called—the Snow Princess? Are you as cold as snow? Shall I call you my little icicle and will you melt in my arms? [*He laughs and rises*] What a situation. [*He draws her to her feet*] Oh, how Marta will laugh.

MUSIC
No. 10

SCENE 6

CRISTIANE. Will she? I wonder.

NIKKI sits on the settee and pulls CRISTIANE on to his knee. She melts in his arms.

LIGHTING CUE 7

The lights fade to BLACK-OUT and the music swells as—

the RUNNING TABS *close*

SCENE 6

Outside the Palace, under the boudoir window

The scene is an inset showing the outside of the boudoir window and its balcony C.

When the RUNNING TABS *open, the* GIPSY SERENADERS, *a quartet of male singers and an instrumentalist, are singing under the window in the moonlight. There is a light in the window and the window curtains are open. They are halfway through the song.*

QUARTET

"MOUNTAIN DOVE"

SERENADERS

No. 11

SERENADERS.
Farewell, my little Mountain Dove
The winds are calling you away.
I too can feel their stern command
That none may disobey.
But you, will you be mindful yet
Will you forget, my little mountain dove?

If this were love,
Deep tender love,
This hour were an hour divine.
If all this were true
Gentle and true
Then earth and heaven would be mine.
The sky would burn with a million stars
And moonlight dance along the sea,
If this were love and I were in your arms
And you were in love with me.

A hand appears and draws the curtains across the window.

LIGHTING CUE 8

The light in the window goes out. The SERENADERS *blow kisses to the window.*

LIGHTING CUE 9

The lights dim to BLACK-OUT as the SERENADERS *exit and*

the RUNNING TABS *close*

SCENE 7

The Ballroom of the Palace

It is a magnificent Baroque room with the main entrance approached by two wide steps c of the back wall. There are three tall draped french windows R and similar windows L. The Ballroom is brilliantly lit by large chandeliers. Two low tables stand one each down R and down L.

When the RUNNING TABS *open the Ballroom is crowded with all fashionable Muvania. They are all dancing. The french windows stand open.* VANESCU *is standing down* R. COUNT EGON STANIEFF *is standing up* R. *He is a good-looking young man of about thirty in the uniform of the Royal Guard. The* MAJOR DOMO *stands in the entrance up* C. *Two* FLUNKEYS *stand one each side of the entrance up* C, *and two* FLUNKEYS *stand one each at two french windows* R. *As the* GUESTS *dance, they sing.*

BALLROOM SCENE   No. 12

CHORUS

CHORUS.   Thrilling enthralling music is calling
                       Dance the night away.
                       Beauty commands us and we must obey.
                       Beauty and love are the lords of the land of delight.
                       They are lords of the night.

At the end of the dance, the MAJOR DOMO *announces.*

MAJOR DOMO.   **Her Majesty Queen Elena.** [*He stands to one side of the entrance up* C]

The GUESTS *form two lines in the shape of a* V.

ELENA *enters* C. *She is followed on by* OLGA *and two* CHAMBERLAINS. *She moves down* C *as the* LADIES *curtsy and the* GENTLEMEN *bow.* VANESCU *crosses to* R *of Elena.*

ELENA.   Vanescu—who is that extremely good-looking man in the Royal Guard uniform?

The 1ST CHAMBERLAIN *escorts* OLGA *down* L. *The* 2ND CHAMBERLAIN *moves up* C *and stands in the corridor.*

VANESCU.   That, Your Majesty, is Count Egon Stanieff.
ELENA.   Stanieff—oh, I knew his father. I might almost have been his mother. It's all right—I wasn't. Send him to talk to me.

*V*ANESCU *moves up* R *to Egon.* ELENA *nods graciously to the Guests.* VANESCU *returns with* EGON. ELENA *gives* EGON *her hand to kiss.* VANESCU *crosses down* R.

I was just telling M'sieu Vanescu that I knew your dear father. Is he well?
EGON.   Considering his age, Your Majesty.
ELENA.   And what is his age, Count Stanieff?
EGON.   He admits to seventy.
ELENA.   Impossible—he was a contemporary of mine.
EGON.   Then, Your Majesty—he cannot be more than forty.
ELENA.   Then you must be ten—you are big for your age. Do you dance? You look as if you do—you must dance with the Princess—but please do not fall in love with her. You may—she's enchanting.
EGON.   I am already in love—Your Majesty.
ELENA.   Since when?
EGON.   Since five minutes ago, Your Majesty.
ELENA.   Your father has taught you well. I shall save the first waltz after supper for you. [*She crosses to Vanescu*]

EGON *crosses to Olga.*

He's charming. We must find him some more duties in the Palace. I think this was a good idea that my son and his bride should meet for the first time in public—it will save embarrassment. They will chat—they will dance and that will be that. Vanescu, he will come, won't he?

SCENE 7 KING'S RHAPSODY

Vanescu. His valet assures me that he is already dressed and in excellent form. MUSIC
Elena. I am relieved—he's so unaccountable—even his return last night. Did you know he'd returned?
Vanescu. I heard this morning.
Elena. Really, Vanescu, you and your secret police. Did she return with him?
Vanescu. I gather he returned on horseback alone.
Elena. Then he's left her in the chalet—she could never ride.
2nd Chamberlain [announcing] Madame Marta Karillos.

ENTRANCE OF MARTA No. 13

Elena, surprised, turns, takes a few steps to c, then turns and crosses to Vanescu. There is mild sensation among the Guests.

Elena [over the music] It's not possible! Vanescu, are you responsible for this?

Marta enters up c and greets friends around the doorway.

Vanescu. Madame, I think you know me well enough.
Elena. Almost too well. If I find out who is responsible for this outrage . . .
Vanescu. I think you will find that His Majesty is responsible.

The Major Domo moves down c.

Major Domo [announcing] Madame Marta Karillos.
Vanescu. A little joke.
Elena. In the worst possible taste. She must be got rid of before the Princess arrives. [She crosses to LC]

Marta moves down c. Elena turns. Marta curtsies.

Welcome to Bledz, Madame Karillos, you have just arrived?

The Major Domo moves up c.

Marta. A few weeks ago, Ma'am.
Elena. And are you staying with us long or settling up your affairs before returning to Paris?
Marta. I settled my affairs in Paris before returning to Murania.
Elena. But won't you find it very quiet here?
Marta. I have my own circle of friends, Ma'am.
Elena. Which you have deserted for tonight. [She turns away] How sad they must be.
Marta. If I receive a Royal Command, Ma'am, I can only obey.
Elena. You've been obeying Royal Commands for far too long.

There is mild sensation among the Guests.

Marta. Ma'am—may I assure you that I was deeply touched at being asked tonight and extremely surprised.
Elena. Then you should have had the good manners to refuse. [She moves two or three steps to L]
Marta. I think, Ma'am, I am not the only person in this room tonight who suffers from lack of manners.
Elena. I deserved that. But your being here is most embarrassing.
Marta. That is the last thing I intend. I shall leave immediately I have paid my respects to Her Royal Highness—I think His Majesty will expect this.
Elena. Vanescu, will you escort Madame Karillos to supper. I should hate her to go away hungry.
Vanescu [crossing to R of Marta] Madame, may I have the honour?

Marta curtsies to Elena, then crosses and exits with Vanescu R.
Elena beckons to Olga, who crosses to her.

Elena. Olga, I am as near fainting as I have ever been in my life.
2nd Chamberlain [announcing] His Majesty the King.

ENTRANCE OF THE KING No. 14

Elena [speaking over the music] My son has often shown bad taste—but this! To ask her here the first time he meets the Princess. It is intolerable.

                                NIKKI *enters up* C *and stands on the steps.* ELENA *crosses to* C,   MUSIC
                                faces up C, *curtsies, then crosses to* RC. *The* MAJOR DOMO
                                moves a little down LC.

MAJOR DOMO [*announcing*] His Majesty the King.

                             The LADIES *curtsy and the* GENTLEMEN *bow.* NIKKI *moves
                             down* C, *acknowledging the greetings.*

NIKKI [*kissing Elena's hand*] Mama, you *are* looking incredibly beautiful.

                             The MAJOR DOMO *moves up* C.

ELENA. Then I must have iron self-control—my face should be distorted with rage.
NIKKI. But why, Mama—hasn't everything gone as you wished?—after all, I might not have turned up at all.
ELENA. That would not have surprised me. Nikki, what have you against Cristiane that you should so humiliate her?
NIKKI. Against Cristiane? What could I have against her, I've never even seen her? By the way, how does she look?
ELENA. Quite ravishing.
NIKKI. Princesses are always ravishing—officially.
ELENA. You must try to be polite. Your first meeting—and I should think your last.
NIKKI. My last?
ELENA. How *could* she stay if she finds out?
NIKKI. Finds out what?
ELENA. This appalling insult—her first official reception. She might have had the decency to stay away—plead illness—anything. [*She turns away*]
NIKKI. Mama, I'm not usually slow-witted but I don't know what you are talking about.
ELENA [*turning*] Do you deny asking Marta Karillos to the Palace tonight?
NIKKI. Marta? Here? [*He looks around*] No, Mama, I never ask Marta to official receptions, they bore her almost more than they bore me. How do you...?
ELENA. Are you speaking the truth?
NIKKI. I never do anything else, it saves time. [*He crosses down* L]
2ND CHAMBERLAIN [*announcing*] Her Royal Highness the Princess Cristiane.

                    ENTRANCE OF PRINCESS CRISTIANE   No. 15

                             CRISTIANE *enters up* C. *She is followed on by* VERA. CRISTIANE
                             is elaborately and exquisitely dressed. The MAJOR DOMO *moves a
                             little down* LC.

MAJOR DOMO [*announcing*] Her Royal Highness the Princess Cristiane.

                             CRISTIANE *moves* C. ELENA *crosses to Cristiane, kisses her and
                             leads her to Nikki.* NIKKI'S *back is to the audience but it shows his
                             feelings and recognition.* CRISTIANE *makes a deep curtsy. He
                             raises her and kisses her hand. He can hardly speak for bewilder-
                             ment and anger.* CRISTIANE *is nervous but is frankly enjoying the
                             situation.*

NIKKI. Exquisitely done.

                             ELENA *and* VERA *move down* RC. *The* MAJOR DOMO *moves up* C.

I regret that my illness has prevented our meeting before, Princess, or may I call you Astrid?
CRISTIANE. As you wish, sir, but as my name is Cristiane I may not hear.
NIKKI. Strange, I could have sworn your name was Astrid.
CRISTIANE. Cristiane, sir.
NIKKI. Cristiane—I see. How strange that we should meet in public for the first time—we must be quite unique in history. Have you brought no entourage, no charming maids-in-waiting?
CRISTIANE. Only one, sir—the Countess Lemainken—may I present her?
NIKKI. But, of course.

                             CRISTIANE *beckons to* VERA. VERA *crosses to Cristiane and
                             curtsies to Nikki.*

And she came all the way from Norseland with you. What devotion. Welcome to Murania, Countess —we hope you will stay long with us.

SCENE 7   KING'S RHAPSODY   MUSIC

VERA. Your Majesty is too gracious.
ELENA [*beckoning to Vera*] Countess . . .
                        VERA *turns and crosses to Elena.*
CRISTIANE [*to Nikki*] Sir . . .
NIKKI. Why so much formality—surely you know my name?
CRISTIANE. As well as you know mine. I took the liberty of sending an invitation to a very old friend of yours. I fear she was—of course—quite unintentionally, left out. I wouldn't like her to be left out. Perhaps someone would present her to me—a Madame Karillos.
NIKKI. Who did you say?
CRISTIANE. Madame Karillos.
NIKKI. And you asked her here tonight?
CRISTIANE. Yes, did I do wrong? You see, I would like to think that an old friend of yours would be a friend of mine.
NIKKI. I'm afraid you and Madame Karillos would have little in common.
CRISTIANE. I think we might have a great deal in common. If she is a friend I shall be happy. If she is an enemy I shall at least know who I am fighting.
NIKKI. I warn you it would be a losing fight.
CRISTIANE. For whom?
NIKKI. For you.
CRISTIANE. Then I hope I shall take my defeat gracefully.
NIKKI. You are very direct.
CRISTIANE. I have never learnt to be anything else.
                   MARTA *and* VANESCU *enter* R. ELENA *sees them and crosses to Cristiane.*
ELENA [*endeavouring to take Cristiane up* C] My dear, there are several people who would like to be presented.
NIKKI. Mama, Cristiane is very anxious to meet one of my oldest and most devoted friends.
                   MARTA *crosses to* C. ELENA *crosses above Cristiane and Nikki to* L. CRISTIANE *turns and faces Marta.*
Madame Karillos, the Princess wishes you to be presented. Princess, may I present Madame Marta Karillos.
                   MARTA *curtsies. She and* CRISTIANE *eye each other.*
CRISTIANE. Madame, I am so happy that you were able to come. I feared that my invitation might have got to you too late.
MARTA. I was charmed to receive it, Your Highness, though a little puzzled. I didn't know you knew of my existence.
CRISTIANE. But, of course. Even in Norseland. We are always so delighted to receive beautiful artistes at the Palace. Perhaps if you could find time to visit me we might have some music.
NIKKI [*to Cristiane*] I have heard that you sing.
CRISTIANE. But only as an amateur. I'm sure Madame Karillos could teach me so much.
MARTA. I think, Your Royal Highness, that I can teach you nothing.
CRISTIANE. Not even endurance?
                   MARTA *crosses down* RC.
NIKKI. Are you by any chance proposing to manage my life?
CRISTIANE. To manage it—oh, no—but I should like to make it as easy as possible.
NIKKI. You have made it quite unendurable.

FINALE—ACT I

DANCE AND REPRISE   No. 16

"SOME DAY MY HEART WILL AWAKE"

CRISTIANE

[*He speaks over the music*] Ah! Music to the rescue as always.
  C

VANESCU [*crossing to* C]   I think, sir, they are waiting for you to lead the dancing.
NIKKI.   But, of course.   [*He crosses above Vanescu to Marta*]   Madame Karillos! Will you honour me?

CRISTIANE *moves down* L.

MARTA.   Oh no, please, sir—the Princess.
NIKKI.   The Princess is on duty—she has to be gracious to a hundred people.
MARTA.   Please . . .
NIKKI.   I'm sure she will forgive me if I am gracious to one.

NIKKI *and* MARTA *commence to waltz*. ALL *curtsy and bow, then join in the dance.*

ELENA [*to Cristiane*]   My child, you were foolish to invite her, but you acted with great dignity.
CRISTIANE.   I wasn't thinking of dignity.
ELENA.   Oh, let us forget this stupid affair—you must have an amusing evening. Count Stanieff! [*She looks around*] Here is Count Stanieff, he is I am told a beautiful dancer.

EGON *bows to Cristiane.*

ELENA *crosses and exits down* R. OLGA *follows her off*. VERA *moves to* R *of Cristiane*.

VERA.   My poor child, you're as white as a sheet.
CRISTIANE.   I'm quite all right—it's just that I meant to do the right thing. I thought he would have seen that and now . . . [*She turns to Egon*] Oh, Count Stanieff, forgive me.

VERA *crosses and exits* R.

EGON.   If Your Highness is dancing, may I have the honour?
CRISTIANE [*on the verge of tears*]   You are too kind.
EGON.   Not kind, Your Highness—blind with fury.
CRISTIANE.   This is a Court Ball, Count Stanieff, emotions are out of place.

EGON *looks embarrassed.*

Oh, don't be rebuked—I didn't mean to rebuke you. Please smile and I shall smile too, and everyone will say, "How gay the Princess is—or how insensitive."
EGON.   They'll never say that.
CRISTIANE.   Oh, I have a champion. I never thought I'd need one.
EGON.   There's not a man in this room that wouldn't run him through the heart for that insult to you.
CRISTIANE.   Count Stanieff, may I remind you that you are talking to his future Queen.
EGON.   Then it's true—you are in love with him.
CRISTIANE.   Yes, Count Stanieff—I am in love with him—and some day—some day . . . [*She sings*]

> Some day my heart will awake
> Some day the morning will break,
> Music will open my eyes,
> Showing the skies
> Golden with rapture.
> Maybe this gentle refrain
> Some day will echo again,
> Bringing my lover's caress
> Bidding my heart say yes.

EGON *takes Cristiane's hand and leads her into the dance as—*

the CURTAIN *falls*

ENTR'ACTE MUSIC   No. 17

ACT II

SCENE I

The drawing-room of Marta's villa on the outskirts of Bledz. Evening

It is a magnificent room, over-elaborately furnished and decorated and is typically Muranian with a slightly Slav influence. There are double doors up C, and down R and two pairs of french windows L overlooking the grounds. A large stove stands in an alcove up R. A console table stands up LC. On the wall over it is a large ornate mirror. A long settee stands L with armchairs above and below it. There are armchairs down R and below the stove. A grand piano and stool stand up RC. There is a long stool below the piano. In the alcove R of the double doors there is a chiffonier set out as a buffet. At night the room is lit by wall candle-brackets up C and R and by a candelabra on the console table up L. The room is carpeted and heavy curtains hang at the windows.

When the CURTAIN rises a voluptuous dance is being performed by six girls of the Royal Muranian Corps de Ballet, for the delight of NIKKI, MARTA, some lady GUESTS and OFFICERS of the Royal Guards. Champagne is being offered round by four MENSERVANTS wearing National costume, and the whole company is gay and slightly tipsy. NIKKI and MARTA are seated on the settee. VOLKOFF is standing down R.

OPENING DANCE   No. 18

DANCERS

The dance ends in a picture.

EXIT MUSIC   No. 18a

The DANCERS *exit.* NIKKI *rises and crosses to* L *of the piano.*

NIKKI. They dance well, Marta—and are quite young. That is usual in the State Opera. You should have them appear with you in Paris, and introduce them into one of your operettas.
MARTA [*rising*] No, sir. [*She crosses to* R] Those young things! I couldn't afford to—the audience already have an idea of my age, I don't want them to be certain.
NIKKI [*moving down* C] Some women never age.
MARTA. A man never says that to a woman until she has.
NIKKI. Marta, I must think that out. Volkoff, any news from the Palace?
VOLKOFF. Not yet, sir. There are six messengers with fast horses waiting on the road, they will pass the message on to each other. You should hear within twenty minutes of the happy event.
NIKKI. I shall hear before that. Don't forget the guns. How many guns for a boy?
VOLKOFF. Twenty-one, sir.
NIKKI. And a girl?
VOLKOFF. Eighteen, sir.
NIKKI. How very unfair, but eventually girls get even, they always do. What a delightful way of approaching fatherhood. I believe the poor husband usually paces up and down and has a raging toothache. I prefer wine, women and song. [*He moves to the piano*] Talking of song—Marta, sing to us.
MARTA [*crossing to* R *of Nikki*] What shall I sing, sir?
NIKKI [*moving down* C] There's a very attractive song I hear everywhere—in the streets—even when I ride into the country, but I have never heard the words clearly. In fact, as I approach, people stop singing it. I wonder what that means.

The GUESTS *exchange embarrassed glances.*

Would you know the song I mean, Marta? It sounds like the Mayor of—some French name?
MARTA. Would it be the *Mayor of Perpignan?*
NIKKI. Perpignan. Yes, that's it, the *Mayor of Perpignan.* Does anyone know it?
MARTA [*moving down* RC] Everyone knows it, sir, but none would be likely to sing it in front of you.
NIKKI. Am I so easily shocked?

MARTA. Well, it's not shocking.
NIKKI. Applicable?
MARTA. I don't think so.
NIKKI. But some people do. You make me more curious than ever. This Mayor of Perpignan—a popular character—I gather not, and is there a Madame la Maire his wife?
MARTA. There is, sir.
NIKKI. And it's all about them. Well, well, now let's hear it.
MARTA. I would prefer not.
NIKKI. Oh, but I insist—in fact, I command. Don't forget that jolly little tune, *The Marseillaise*—it started a revolution. This might start another one. How amusing. [*He crosses and sits in the armchair down* L

VOLKOFF *moves up* RC *and sits at the piano.*

MARTA. But don't say I didn't warn you.

SONG   No. 19

"THE MAYOR OF PERPIGNAN"

MARTA *and* CHORUS

LIGHTING CUE 10

The lights dim with the exception of a spot focused on Marta.

MARTA.   The Mayor of Perpignan
         Had a wife;
         And the whole of Perpignan
         Loved the wife of the
         Mayor of Perpignan
         But they never loved the
         Mayor of Perpignan.

MEN.   Now the Mayor of Perpignan
         Had a wife;
         And the whole of Perpignan
         Loved the wife of the
         Mayor of Perpignan
         But they never loved the
         Mayor of Perpignan.

MARTA.   Oh, Madame la Maire
         Everybody loves her badly.
         Every time she raises her sky-blue eyes
         Their hearts beat madly.
         Oh, Madame la Maire
         Never let your husband know
         That the cheers he hears
         In the street when we meet
         Are all for Madame la Maire,
         Not the Mayor of Perpignan.

CHORUS. Oh, Madame la Maire
         Everybody loves her badly.
         Every time she raises her sky-blue eyes
         Their hearts beat madly.

| | Oh, Madame la Maire
Never let your husband know
That the cheers he hears
In the street when we meet
Are all for Madame la Maire,
Not for the Mayor of Perpignan. |
|---|---|
| MARTA. | Now the Mayor of Perpignan
Had a son
And the whole of Perpignan
Knew the son of the
Mayor of Perpignan
Wasn't very like the
Mayor of Perpignan. |
| MEN. | Now the Mayor of Perpignan
Had a son
And the whole of Perpignan
Knew the son of the
Mayor of Perpignan
Wasn't very like the
Mayor of Perpignan. |
| MARTA. | Oh, Madame la Maire
Smile upon the town so sweetly
No-one ever dreamed that she could behave
So indiscreetly.
Oh, Madame la Maire
Never let your husband know
That his only son
And his only one
Belongs to Madame la Maire,
Not the Mayor of Perpignan. |
| CHORUS. | Oh, Madame la Maire
Never let your husband know
That his only son
And his only one
Belongs to Madame la Maire,
Not the Mayor of Perpignan. |

LIGHTING CUE 11

The lights come up.

NIKKI. But that was charming. And so gloriously disloyal. But why were you so tentative about singing it? A little song about a provincial French Mayor and his wife. How could it offend me?

The boom of a gun is heard off in the distance. The gunfire continues at spaced intervals until twenty-one shots have been fired.

VOLKOFF [*rising and crossing to the upstage window* L] The guns, sir.

NIKKI [*rising*] So it is. Welcome little Prince or Princess. Will someone count for me? I could never count up to more than ten—eleven if given a chocolate.

VOLKOFF. That is four, sir.

NIKKI. Four. They must be using two guns. Strange that silly booming noise is telling us our future. They'll like a boy—they'll only tolerate a girl—and why? *Women* are so much stronger than men—the weaker vessel, nonsense! I suppose, Volkoff, the populace pictures me at the bedside, where officially I am.

MARTA. I should hate them to know where you really are. My life wouldn't be worth a copec.   MUSIC
NIKKI. Yes, the Queen has a great following, as her stock goes up, mine goes down—but then she always does the right thing—I always do the wrong.
VOLKOFF. Seventeen, sir.
NIKKI. And now shall we listen quietly?

There is silence in the room until the gunfire ceases.

A boy!
VOLKOFF [*crossing to Nikki*] May I be the first to congratulate you, sir?

The GUESTS crowd around Nikki and congratulate him. MARTA crosses quietly to the downstage window L and stands gazing out.

NIKKI. This calls for a celebration—some music. How about the National Anthem—such a good tune. Does anyone know it?

There are cries of "Oh, yes, sir" and general laughter. The National Anthem of Murania is sung unaccompanied.

"THE NATIONAL ANTHEM OF MURANIA" No. 20

CHORUS

ALL. Dear land of Song
And Liberty
We hymn thy ancient name.
Thy songs are strong
And true to thee,
The champions of thy fame.
From age to age
Thy heritage
Shall proudly dwell secure
On heath and hill
Thy spirit still,
Undaunted, shall endure.

NIKKI. Thank you, gentlemen. I find myself strangely moved for the first time. I wonder why? [*He crosses to Marta*] Now, something gayer. [*He draws* MARTA *to* C] The *Mayor of Perpignan* again.
MARTA. No. No!

VOLKOFF *crosses and sits at the piano.*

NIKKI. It's more applicable than ever.

REPRISE No. 20a

"THE MAYOR OF PERPIGNAN"

MARTA *and* CHORUS

Oh! Madame la Maire
Smiled upon the town so sweetly
No-one ever dreamed that she could behave
So indiscreetly.
Oh! Madame la Maire
Never let your husband know
That his only son
And his only one
Belongs to Madame la Maire,
Not the Mayor of Perpignan.

> *The song ceases abruptly as the doors up* C *are suddenly flung open revealing* ELENA *on the threshold. There is a short silence.* MARTA *curtsies.*   MUSIC

NIKKI [*moving to Elena*] My dearest Mother, what an honour, but why? [*He leads Elena down* C] Oh, I know, you've come to fetch me home.
ELENA. Dismiss your friends.
NIKKI. If you wish it, Mama. Ladies, gentlemen, fellow officers, you are dismissed but only temporarily.

> *The* OFFICERS *bow, the* LADIES *curtsy and all exit up* C *and* L. VOLKOFF *exits up* C. MARTA *curtsies and turns to go but* ELENA *stops her.*

ELENA. No, Marta, stay and hear what I have to say. Please be seated.

> MARTA *sits on the settee.*

I thought you had influence—in some ways quite a good one, and yet the night his child is born, you lure him to your house.
MARTA. It was not my wish, ma'am.
NIKKI [*moving between Elena and Marta*] No, Mama, entirely mine. I utterly refuse to play in the charade—I do not feel the slightest emotion. Why should I pretend to? And you, Mama, what are you feeling at this moment?
ELENA. Tremendous relief.
NIKKI. Yes, I see what you mean. You can focus attention on your grandson instead of concentrating on your son's nocturnal activities.
ELENA. You make me very unhappy, Nikki. Why are you so bitter?
NIKKI. Because I've been used, everything has led up to today. Everything Cristiane and you have worked for has come true—there's an heir and God help poor Nikki! [*He crosses down* R] Just a word of warning, Mama—don't under-estimate Cristiane, she's made of cold steel. I shan't fight you, I'm too tired—but she's not, she's young and strong and the people adore her. They're tired of us, with our lovers and mistresses, we're old-fashioned, Mama, but she's new, the latest thing, a good woman. [*He sits in the armchair down* R]
ELENA [*crossing to* L *of Nikki*] What do you want, Nikki?
NIKKI. At the moment, I have a strong desire to see my son, that small piece of humanity which has been designed to push his father off the throne. I wonder which it will be—exile or assassination, Mama?
ELENA. Don't, Nikki. [*She crosses to Marta*] Marta, speak to him.
MARTA [*rising*] Sir—you said just now you had a strong desire to see your son. I think you should go immediately to the Palace and show yourself on the balcony with the little Prince.
NIKKI. Yes, and if I had any sense, I'd drop him over.
ELENA. Nikki!
NIKKI. But I haven't any sense. Very good, Mama—one last bid for popularity. [*He rises and escorts* ELENA *to the doors up* C, *then turns to Marta*] Good night, Marta, my dear. As always you've given me a delightful evening.

> ELENA *exits up* C.

MARTA [*moving to Nikki*] And shall I see you?
NIKKI. Constantly—nothing has changed.
MARTA. I wish I could be sure. Good night, sir.
NIKKI. How long is it? Over twenty years, twenty years on a precipice. Women are wonderful creatures.

END OF SCENE MUSIC   No. 21

> NIKKI *exits up* C. MARTA *crosses to the settee, sits on it and weeps as—*
>
> *the* RUNNING TABS *close*
>
> *The music continues.*

SCENE 2

The drawing-room of Marta's villa. Six months later. Late afternoon

The music fades.

When the RUNNING TABS *open a* MANSERVANT *is showing* CRISTIANE, EGON *and* VERA *into the room.*

MANSERVANT [*bowing deeply*] If Your Majesty would care to wait—Madame assured me she would return home by five.
CRISTIANE. Well, then—we'll wait—it is after half past four now.
MANSERVANT. May I offer Your Majesty a little refreshment? I fear the household is a little upset.
CRISTIANE. Of course it is, nothing upsets a household more than impending departure.
MANSERVANT. Madame Karillos' decision to leave was so sudden, Your Majesty. I will inform her that you are here directly she returns.
CRISTIANE. Thank you, you may leave us now.

The MANSERVANT *bows and exits up* C. EGON *stands* L *of the piano.* VERA *moves down* C.

[*She crosses slowly down* R *and looks around*] This house has charm—the Palace has none. Yes, I see why he liked to come here. Oh, Egon, don't look so gloomy.
EGON. Ma'am, I am gloomy, this is a very dangerous thing to do.
CRISTIANE. Why dangerous? We go for a little drive into the country, I see a charming villa—what could be more natural than I should want to see the inside, and if Madame Karillos has "callers" . . .
VERA. Yes, callers with knives and guns.
CRISTIANE. Which they would hardly dare use in my presence.
EGON. These people are fanatics. If they wish to dispose of her they won't care who stands in their way.
CRISTIANE. Even the Queen they love so dearly—for the moment. [*She crosses to the piano*] Oh, Egon, I think my way is best. [*She sits on the stool below the piano*] Now, what shall we do while we're waiting? Look at photograph albums—or is that too banal? A little music perhaps; music has always played a big part in this house—it might soothe the feelings of any—passers-by.
VERA [*crossing and sitting on the settee*] You should have put a guard round the house.
CRISTIANE. And precipitate a crisis? No, I still think my way is best. [*She rises and turns to the piano*] Oh, look, here are all her songs—[*she picks up the music*] some dedicated to her by the composer. *Qu'as-tu fait de mon cœur*—now that means "What have you done to my heart." What indeed? Tosti's *Goodbye*—how appropriate. *The Gates of Paradise.* We all know that—"Fling wide the Gates of Paradise and let the glory of the dawn break through." Not a bad idea—though a little optimistic perhaps. Egon—Vera—come, and we'll all sing and it will sound so peaceful and domestic.

TRIO   No. 22

"THE GATES OF PARADISE"

CRISTIANE, VERA *and* EGON

CRISTIANE *sits at the piano.* VERA *rises, crosses and stands* R *of Cristiane.*

EGON.
    Sweet love, with you beside me
    Till night has flown once more,
    Whatever fortune may hold in store
    We'll send our echoes from shore to shore.
    I watch the far horizon
    For signs that dawn is near
    But still the darkness is deep and drear
    Where silver glimmers will soon appear.

SCENE 2   KING'S RHAPSODY

MUSIC

CRISTIANE.	Fling wide the gates of Paradise And let the glory of the dawn break through. Fling wide the gates of Paradise And let the longings of the world come true.
EGON.	Bring beauty to our weary eyes And let the happy Golden Age begin.
CRISTIANE and EGON.	Fling wide the gates of Paradise That every loving heart may enter in.
VERA.	Fling wide the gates of Paradise And let the glory of the dawn break through. Fling wide the gates of Paradise And let the longings of the world come true. Bring beauty to our weary eyes And let the happy Golden Age begin. Fling wide the gates of Paradise That every loving heart may enter in.
ALL.	Fling wide the gates of Paradise And let the glory of the dawn break through. Fling wide the gates of Paradise And let the longings of the world come true. Bring beauty to our weary eyes And let the happy Golden Age begin. Fling wide the gates of Paradise That every loving heart may enter in.

After the applause they commence the encore.

ALL.	Fling wide the gates of Paradise And let the glory of the dawn break through. Fling wide the gates of Paradise And let the longings of the world come true.

NIKKI enters up C. *Only* EGON *sees him.* NIKKI *motions him to take no notice and the song continues.*

Bring beauty to our weary eyes
And let the happy Golden Age begin.
Fling wide the gates of Paradise
That every loving heart may enter in.

There is a silence. CRISTIANE *looks up and sees Nikki.*

NIKKI [*after a pause*] Count Stanieff, will you escort Countess Lemainken to the other room.

EGON *bows.* VERA *curtsies and exits up* C. EGON *follows her off.*

And what does this gesture mean?
   CRISTIANE [*rising*] Gesture?
   NIKKI [*moving* LC] Yes, gesture. I don't seem to remember meeting you here before—and on today of all days.
   CRISTIANE. Shall we call it a formal visit of farewell?
   NIKKI. My God, you're clever—you engineer the whole thing—make her position here intolerable and you put yourself completely in the right by calling on her.
   CRISTIANE. I have engineered nothing. Madame Karillos has realized a little late that her presence in Murania is no longer to be tolerated. [*She sits on the stool below the piano*]
   NIKKI. And why? Because of you. My people have got to have someone to idolize, I've let them down, so they turn to you—the saint, the people's friend, the mother.

CRISTIANE. Of your son, Nikki. [*She pauses*] I see you're not interested. Very well, then. During the last year Madame Karillos has sent five million roubles out of this country—she will live in the utmost luxury, and who will pay?—the people—whose friend I am.
NIKKI. Are you giving me any news? Do you think I don't know? [*He crosses to the window and gazes out*] She's not making provision for herself—she's making it for me—for us.
CRISTIANE [*rising*] You and she—oh, no!
NIKKI. Yes, she goes tonight, quite publicly, and in a few weeks—I shall slip out of the country and that will be the end of that.
CRISTIANE. No, never the end—[*she crosses to him*] not with you alive.
NIKKI. I don't propose to die for you—or your party.
CRISTIANE. Nikki, it's very hard for me to ask you for anything—but I've got to; don't do this—don't let the past kill the future. You've had your life—you and she. Stay here—oh, not for my sake but for your son's.

NIKKI *sits on the settee.*

You pretend not to be wise, but you are—you can guide him. You love him—you know you do—and he adores you already. Think of his life—a little boy surrounded by cruel ruthless men—I shall be helpless. [*She sits above Nikki on the settee*] Oh, Nikki, think—please, please. [*She weeps*]
NIKKI [*rising*] Is it possible that you are, after all, human?
CRISTIANE. Have you ever tried to find out?
NIKKI [*crossing to* C, *turning and facing her*] I've thought you ambitious, scheming . . .
CRISTIANE. I've never schemed.
NIKKI. You trapped me once.
CRISTIANE. It was my only way.
NIKKI. But why?
CRISTIANE. Oh, you fool! You fool! [*She turns away from him*]
NIKKI. Cristiane, tell me why.
CRISTIANE. Can't you see, can't you see?
NIKKI. It's not possible.

EGON *enters up* C.

EGON. Forgive me, Your Majesty, but Madame Karillos is here in great distress. Her carriage was attacked. Countess Lemainken is attending her.
NIKKI. Good God!
CRISTIANE. So it happened. I knew I was right to come.
MARTA [*off up* C] I must get to the King.

MARTA *enters up* C. CRISTIANE *rises.* EGON *exits up* C.

Sir, I have had a most terrible experience. [*She curtsies*] Ma'am.
NIKKI. Could you bear to tell us what exactly happened?
MARTA. As you know, I was leaving here for Bucharest tonight—everyone knew it—I had some farewell calls to make. I had an ominous feeling all day and just now when my carriage got to the top of the hill, some roughs appeared with knives and sticks shouting horrible abuses. My coachman and footman were both armed and kept them off while I scrambled from the carriage. I've never been openly attacked before and I'm deathly afraid—such hatred I've never realized before.
NIKKI. Forget it, Marta. By tomorrow morning you will be safe across the frontier. By the way, you must join the train at Hervat. It will be safer. I must tell Stanieff to arrange that.
MARTA. I loved my house. I was happy here.
NIKKI. And you will be happy again. Think, Marta—Paris—all your friends. Not like the old days when you had to sing to keep yourself—yes, and me too.
MARTA. How long shall I be alone?
NIKKI. How do you mean—alone?
MARTA. May I repeat my question? How long shall I be alone?
NIKKI. You could never be alone for long.
MARTA. Are you wilfully misunderstanding me?

EGON *enters excitedly up* C.

EGON. Sir, they've broken into the grounds of the villa—they've killed two of the guard. You must leave immediately—I am responsible for Her Majesty's safety.
NIKKI. No, Stanieff, I am responsible for Her Majesty's safety.
EGON. But, sir! They threaten to burn the place down and everybody in it.

> MARTA *crosses to Cristiane. The sounds of the approaching crowd are heard.*

I implore you, sir, in two minutes it will be too late, they're surrounding the house.
NIKKI. What a charming story that would make. " The King and Queen slink away from hysterical peasants." Pull yourself together, Stanieff.

> *The noise of the crowd is heard nearer.*

MARTA [*pushing Cristiane towards the door*] Sir, please go.
NIKKI [*moving between Cristiane and Marta*] I want you to do exactly as I say—go into the next room and wait there.
CRISTIANE. And you?
NIKKI. I shall stay here.
MARTA. But you'll be alone.
NIKKI. Stanieff will stay with me. Please do as I say—yes, Cristiane, you too.

> CRISTIANE *and* MARTA *cross and exit* R.

And now, Stanieff, relax.
EGON. But how can I, sir? [*He moves the armchair from up* L *and places it against the doors as if to barricade them*]
NIKKI. I don't know, but do. And for God's sake take that ridiculous chair away. The doors open the other way, anyway.

> EGON *replaces the chair.*

They may think better of it, but if they come, don't be provoked by anything they may say or do. [*He looks off* L] Yes, I think someone is climbing the balcony. [*Very casually*] And where were you thinking of spending your leave?
EGON. My leave, sir?
NIKKI. You will probably join your father. By the way, how is he?

> *Three* ROUGHS, *in peasant clothes, enter through the french windows* L.

Oh, we seem to have visitors. [*To the Roughs*] What is the meaning of this interruption? Do you usually enter private houses by climbing balconies? This *is* a private house, by the way.
1ST ROUGH. Yes, we know—the Harlot's house.
NIKKI. Is it? And I've been coming here for years—someone might have told me. By the way, why aren't you kneeling?
2ND ROUGH. We've done with kneeling.
NIKKI. I think not—you will kneel in chains for the rest of your lives for this outrage—or perhaps it isn't an outrage, just a friendly call. [*He crosses to* RC] If so, why these glowering looks? Have you a grievance? Some petition you wish to present? [*He pauses*] Tell me, don't be tongue-tied.
1ST ROUGH. We've come here to do a job.
2ND ROUGH. A job that should have been done long ago.
NIKKI. I know, but the shortage of labour . . .
3RD ROUGH. He's talking like this to gain time.
1ST ROUGH. We mean no harm to you.
NIKKI. I'm so relieved—then who are you threatening?
1ST ROUGH. An enemy of the Queen.
NIKKI. Has she an enemy?
3RD ROUGH. She's got an enemy and we know her name—Karillos.
1ST ROUGH. Hand her over—we'll deal with her. Karillos! We spit on her. Isn't the Queen good enough for you?
NIKKI. Far too good, my friend. Do you know what it is like to be fed with lies—it's an upsetting diet—hence this lack of control.

1ST ROUGH. We know lies when we hear them.
NIKKI. But do you know the truth?
1ST ROUGH. We know one truth—you and your Karillos are breaking the Queen's heart.
NIKKI. Breaking the Queen's heart—what a nauseating sentence. Funny, she never told me her heart was breaking. I must ask her about it. [*He crosses to the door* R, *opens it and calls*] My dear, have you a moment?

The ROUGHS, *puzzled, look at each other.*

CRISTIANE *and* MARTA *enter* R. CRISTIANE *has her arm around* MARTA *and they are both smiling.*

CRISTIANE [*apparently not seeing the Roughs*] I was just making a list of the things I've asked Marta to bring me from Paris. She says . . . [*She looks at the Roughs*] Oh, you're busy—another time. [*She turns to go*]

The ROUGHS *look stunned.*

NIKKI. My dear—would you answer me a simple question—is your heart breaking?
CRISTIANE. My heart breaking? What is this—some joke?
NIKKI. I should have thought so, but my friends here think not. Tell me, is it true—is your heart breaking?
CRISTIANE. That's a strong word. I'm sad, naturally—one is always sad when a good friend goes away—and she's sad, too—aren't you, Marta? Oh, please, what does all this mean? Surely our last evening all together could have been private?
1ST ROUGH [*turning to his comrades*] We are being fooled.
NIKKI [*crossing to* C] No, not now—but I think you've been very much fooled in the past. Oh, don't think I don't know the malicious lies that have been spread about Madame Karillos—but they are only political. Oh, Cristiane, I think you can explain better than I exactly what Marta means to all of us.
CRISTIANE. Perhaps I can. [*To the Roughs*] I think you trust me, you always have. You have my word that as far as I am concerned Madame Karillos is a valued and faithful friend, and if I could persuade her to stay in Murania I should do so. And now please go to your homes—the King and I will try to forget this ever happened. Oh, don't worry—I shall even forget your faces, and I am sure the King will, too.
NIKKI. I shall try, but it will be difficult.

The ROUGHS *turn towards the french windows.*

No, don't use the balcony—you might break your necks and I should hate that to happen. The front door this time—Count Stanieff will show you the way.

The ROUGHS *exit up* C. EGON *follows them off.*

Now what are these extravagant plans . . .? Thank you, Cristiane, that was finely done.
MARTA. I am grateful, Ma'am, it was a big gesture—I almost wish you hadn't made it.

NIKKI *crosses to the window and looks out.*

NIKKI. They're dispersing—they seem satisfied—but for how long? [*He turns*] Marta, if you are to get to Hervat in time you must start now—this minute—the drive is a good sixty miles. Stanieff is to escort you.
MARTA. Yes—I realize I must be on my way and the sooner the better, but, Ma'am—could I have just a minute alone with you?
NIKKI [*smiling*] But, of course. But, Marta—don't give me away. She thinks I'm a bad character —don't disillusion her.

NIKKI *crosses and exits* R.

MARTA. Ma'am—I want to tell you something in two minutes that would ordinarily take a lifetime. It's about him and me—he's never been loved—until now, except by me. I think it's that made him afraid—everything he wasn't meant to be. He used me to gain his freedom and I've always meant that to him—freedom It's more than that really—I'm his youth—the youth he never had.

CRISTIANE *crosses and sits in the armchair down* L.

We were happy all those years—and when he decided to come back he also clung to the shreds of hap-

piness that remained. He wanted to be King—he also wanted me—he thought it would work. It might
have, but he fell in love.
CRISTIANE. He fell in love?
MARTA. Oh yes, he fell in love for the first time. I knew it instantly, but of course, being a woman
I wouldn't recognize it. [*She crosses to* LC *and kneels*] So, Ma'am, that is my—explanation—also my
apology.

                                CRISTIANE *rises.*

I beg you to accept it and please forgive me for robbing you of a whole precious year of happiness.
    CRISTIANE [*raising Marta*] Do you know—in a strange way I'm grateful to you. This year has
taught me more than ten years of happiness. I wasn't ready—perhaps I am now—I hope so.

                                NIKKI *enters* R.

    NIKKI. Have I come in too soon?
    MARTA No—just at the right time. I'd finished all I had to say. In fact, there's only one thing
more to say——
                           CRISTIANE *turns away to the window.*
—[*she crosses to Nikki*] the saddest word of all—forgive me if I don't say it—I should find it too difficult.
                       MARTA *drops into a deep curtsy, then exits up* C. CRISTIANE,
                               weeping a little, moves up LC.
    NIKKI [*crossing to Cristiane*] You're crying?
    CRISTIANE. Not for myself.
    NIKKI. For her?
    CRISTIANE. Of course.
    NIKKI. Now that this excitement seems to have died down, may we resume our conversation?
    CRISTIANE [*moving down* LC] Our conversation?
    NIKKI. I asked you why you tricked me and you called me a fool.
    CRISTIANE. I am still calling you a fool. A blind, blind fool!
    NIKKI [*moving to* R *of her*] Blind! Oh, it's not possible. You've got everything you want now.
    CRISTIANE. Not quite. I've got a memory, a drunken King making love to his bride's maidservant.
It sounds squalid, doesn't it? But not to me. I wanted you from the moment I wanted anything—[*she
turns her back to him*] and I quite shamelessly want you still.
    NIKKI. Cristiane—look at me.
                                CRISTIANE *turns.*
Are you telling me that in spite of everything, my appalling behaviour, you think—you—I can hardly say
the word—love me?
    CRISTIANE. No more, no less than I have always loved you.
    NIKKI. But you've never even looked at me. I hardly know the colour of your eyes.
    CRISTIANE. And what colour are they?
    NIKKI [*moving close to her*] Much bluer and deeper than they've any right to be. [*He takes her in
his arms and fiercely kisses her*] This is fantastic. A pair of blue eyes and a year of suspicion and hatred
is wiped out. No, it's too easy, there must be something behind it.
    CRISTIANE. Oh, stop doubting.
    NIKKI. And why shouldn't I doubt? Just cast your mind back to that disgraceful evening. I—
very drunkenly and very caddishly tell my fiancée's maid that my marriage is—to put it politely—a marriage in name only, and what happens—I get seduced.
    CRISTIANE. You . . .
    NIKKI. Oh yes, I get seduced, and why? Because there's got to be an heir—and the next night this
maid walks into the ballroom and says, " You see the girl you made love to is your Princess. Now let's
all settle down and have fun." So we did settle down, but we didn't have fun—at least I didn't. Oh,
this year! How I've hated you and how I've longed for *Astrid*.
    CRISTIANE. That shameless hussy of a maid of mine. I shall dismiss her.
    NIKKI. And I shall sneak her up the back stairs.
    CRISTIANE. When?

NIKKI. Tonight. This is going to be a shock for a lot of people. Mama . . .
CRISTIANE. God protect us!
NIKKI. And the faithful Egon. By the way, is he your lover?
CRISTIANE. Certainly not.
NIKKI. Then he must be mad.
CRISTIANE. And if he were my lover?
NIKKI. Darling, I know so many ways of killing people.
CRISTIANE. Are you happy?
NIKKI. Happy. Is that some new word?
CRISTIANE. Do you like the sound of it?
NIKKI. Happy. Yes, I think I do. Perhaps it's the word I've been looking for all my life.

REPRISE

"THE GATES OF PARADISE"

No. 22a

VERA

As the music commences NIKKI *and* CRISTIANE, *hand in hand, exit by the french windows* L.

VERA *enters up* C *and moves down* C.

VERA.   Fling wide the gates of Paradise
And let the longings of the world come true.
Bring beauty to our weary eyes
And let the happy Golden Age begin.
Fling wide the gates of Paradise
That every loving heart may enter in.

CURTAIN

ENTR'ACTE MUSIC

No. 23

ACT III

Scene i

The Garden of the Summer Palace at Kalacz. A year later

A colonnade fills the back of the stage. There are exits R and L. In the distance can be seen the small Castle, a little-used country residence belonging to Nikki, which he has kept completely rural. Everyone dresses in peasant costume and there is a very friendly country atmosphere. Nikki and Cristiane regard themselves as private citizens and there is no formality. Elena, on her best behaviour, is staying at the Castle, and amateur theatricals are in the air.

When the CURTAIN *rises,* VERA, *wearing peasant costume, is* C, *surrounded by the* CHORUS *and* DANCERS *all in peasant costume.*

SONG AND BALLET No. 24

"TAKE YOUR GIRL"

VERA, CHORUS *and* DANCERS

VERA.
Johnnie was shy
Never dared wink an eye
At the prettiest girl he'd ever seen.
Johnnie was proud
Never dared say aloud
That he loved her and wanted her for Queen.

So at last Johnnie flew
Crying: "What shall I do?"
To his mother, a dame who was wise.
Johnnie was gay
On that red letter day
When she gave him the sweetest of replies.

Take your girl
For the cherries on her lips
For the cherries on her lips
Take your girl
Take your girl.
For the peaches in her cheeks
For the peaches in her cheeks
Take your girl.
She's the girl
With the sunlight in her hair
With the sunlight in her hair
She's the girl.
Take your girl
For a honeymoon in June,
June's the time for honeymoon,
Take your girl.

VERA *moves from* C *in accordance with the dance, which follows later.*

CHORUS.
Take your girl
For the cherries on her lips
For the cherries on her lips
Take your girl.

```
              Take your girl
              For the peaches in her cheeks
              For the peaches in her cheeks
              Take your girl.
              She's the girl
              With the sunlight in her hair
              With the sunlight in her hair
              She's the girl.
              Take your girl
              For a honeymoon in June,
              June's the time for honeymoon,
              Take your . . .
              Ah!

   [Spoken]   Johnny! Johnny! Johnny! Johnny!
```

The dance follows. At the end of the dance the CHORUS *sing a reprise.*

CHORUS.   Take your girl
           For the cherries on her lips
           For the cherries on her lips
           Take your girl.
           Take your girl
           For the peaches in her cheeks
           For the peaches in her cheeks
           Take your girl.
           She's the girl
           With the sunlight in her hair
           With the sunlight in her hair
           She's the girl.
           Take your girl
           For a honeymoon in June,
           June's the time for honeymoon,
           Take your girl.

   [Spoken]   Johnny! Johnny!

The dance ends in a picture. The CHORUS *sing an encore.*

CHORUS.   Take your girl
           For the cherries on her lips
           For the cherries on her lips
           Take your girl.
           Take your girl
           For the peaches in her cheeks
           For the peaches in her cheeks
           Take your girl.
           She's the girl
           With the sunlight in her hair
           With the sunlight in her hair
           She's the girl.
           Take your girl
           For a honeymoon in June,
           June's the time for honeymoon,
           Take your girl.

BASSES.	Take your girl For the cherries on her lips For the cherries on her lips Take your girl. Take your girl For the peaches in her cheeks For the peaches in her cheeks Take your girl.	MUSIC
ALL.	She's the girl With the sunlight in her hair With the sunlight in her hair She's the girl. Take your girl For a honeymoon in June, June's the time for honeymoon, Take your girl.	
	[*Spoken*] Johnny! Johnny!	

At the end of the number ALL *exit and the lights dim quickly to* BLACK-OUT.

LIGHTING CUE 12

MELOS

No. 24a

During the BLACK-OUT *and Melos music a garden table and three wicker chairs are set down* L.

LIGHTING CUE 13

The lights come up.
NIKKI *and* ELENA *enter* R *and cross to* C.

ELENA. I must say it's very charming here. I think I could stand it for about a week. Charming!
NIKKI [*crossing to* L] Why don't you?
ELENA. My dear Nikki, just because you are being a country Squire on his honeymoon, it doesn't mean that we can all sit around and twiddle our thumbs. [*She crosses and sits* R *of the table*] I have brought down a whole pile of papers for you to sign and you won't even look at them. Oh, no, it must be picnics, expeditions, private theatricals and poor Murania must govern itself.
NIKKI [*sitting* L *of the table*] If only you would let it, Mama.
ELENA. I—my dear boy—I'm just a pensioner—nobody takes any notice of me—time was. I don't know what I'm going to do.
NIKKI. I think you've a pretty good idea what you're going to do. Hervat—a new castle with a hundred bedrooms and fifty thousand acres—your own Court, in fact.
ELENA. And why not? It only needs your signature.
NIKKI. Which it will never get. That estate is being given back to the peasants who planted it two hundred years ago.
ELENA. You must be mad—they'd let it go to rack and ruin in a month.
NIKKI. Not if they owned it.
ELENA. You'd give it to them?
NIKKI. Unconditionally.
ELENA. Then I know exactly where I am.
NIKKI. I wish I knew exactly where you are. Furthermore, by way of celebration, they are going to dance a Muranian Rhapsody here.
ELENA. You'd have them here?

CRISTIANE *enters* R.

Peasants in the Castle?
NIKKI. Certainly.

D

ELENA. I shall appeal to Cristiane—she'll be on my side. [*She calls*] Cristiane! MUSIC
CRISTIANE [*crossing to* C] Yes, Mother Elena?
ELENA [*rising and crossing to* L *of Cristiane*] Tell Nikki not to be ridiculous about Hervat, or perhaps you don't know anything about it?
CRISTIANE. I know everything about it, and I think he's perfectly right.
ELENA. How odious of you. [*She kisses Cristiane*] Good morning, darling. Oh dear, why did I have to choose a daughter-in-law with a character? There were several idiotic princesses who would have been clay in my hands. Oh well, I have my friends.

CRISTIANE *crosses to* LC.

NIKKI. Stop intriguing, Mama, or I shall have you exiled.
ELENA. Like poor Marta—I must write to her. We might set up house together in Paris. How amusing.
NIKKI. As you grow older, Mama, your tastes grow worse and worse.
ELENA. Poor Nikki—still hankering. Cristiane, you should put a stop to this—it might develop. Habit is strong.
NIKKI. I think it might be a good idea, Mama, if after all you returned to the Capital. You're far too wicked for us.
ELENA. A reformed character! How dull. What's the time?
CRISTIANE [*sitting* R *of the table*] Nearly eleven.
ELENA. Heavens! My masseur has been waiting an hour. He's quite attractive, tells me all the gossip while he pummels me into unconsciousness. You should try him, Cristiane. I thought in that white gown you seemed to have put on a tiny bit of weight—yes. What time is this ghastly performance?
CRISTIANE. Directly after dinner.
ELENA. I hope it will be good. It ought to be. You've all worked so hard—almost like professionals, but you're not, are you? No, you're not.

ELENA *crosses and exits* R.

NIKKI [*rising and moving up* C] Poor Mama—so afraid—she's finding it very difficult taking second place. [*He turns*] She could have done it so peacefully.
CRISTIANE. Don't do anything drastic.
NIKKI [*moving down* C] About her wild extravagance? Oh, my darling, I've got to—she could ruin us. Every bit of ground we've gained—she can lose it for us.
CRISTIANE. She's still very powerful.
NIKKI. With the older regime. Yes, I grant you that, but dearest, the older regime is passing, and why not? They're a hundred years behind the times. Oh, I know we're a little country, but there's no reason why we shouldn't be well run—a little more for the majority and a little less for the privileged.
CRISTIANE. In our lifetime?
NIKKI [*crossing to* R *of her*] No—but in young Paul's.
CRISTIANE. Have you any plans?
NIKKI. Yes, I have—a big one. [*He takes a document from his pocket*] That's what I have been working on lately. I've called it—for the moment—*The People's Rights*.
CRISTIANE. *The People's Rights*.
NIKKI. I shall force it through the Assembly. They'll kick like steers—but I think I'll get it through.
CRISTIANE. And if you don't?
NIKKI. I shall threaten to abdicate.
CRISTIANE. But if they take you seriously . . .
NIKKI. My dear, they've never taken me seriously. Cristiane, if anything were to happen to me—hold on to young Paul—hold on with all your strength. Don't give an inch. Promise.
CRISTIANE. But what could happen?
NIKKI. I might go too far with my reforms—or too quickly. They're a hard obstinate lot—— [*he crosses to* C]

CRISTIANE *rises and crosses to* L *of Nikki*.

—the older regiment, and they'll fight like hell for their privileges. There, that's enough of the outside world—it does encroach sometimes, doesn't it? I'm so dependent on you. You're so wise. Why are you so wise—after all, it isn't long since you came here? Were you afraid?

CRISTIANE. Terribly. I felt so alone—I nearly gave up. In fact, that night if you had not come to me . . .
NIKKI. Yes—and very charming I was when I did come. I wonder that didn't decide you right away.

SONG   No. 25

"THE VIOLIN BEGAN TO PLAY"

CRISTIANE

CRISTIANE [*over the music*] It did. I realized that I was beaten—and then—and then—a violin began to play. [*She sings*]

And then a violin began to play
Then all my doubts and fears were borne away.
[*She moves down* C]

The RUNNING TABS *close behind Cristiane*

The music carried me to realms far above
Where I knew the meaning of love.
Safe in your arms at last
No more to part
Sweet tears of happiness awoke my heart.
My darkest night was turned into day
When the violin began to play.

I come here as a stranger
And as a stranger I thought to stay
No loving arms to greet me
No loyalty to meet me
As I wandered on my way.
My homeland was calling
Her voices seemed to say:
Come home, come home, come home
But then a violin began to play.

And then a violin began to play
Then all my doubts and fears were borne away
The music carried me to realms far above
Where I knew the meaning of love.
Safe in your arms at last
No more to part
Sweet tears of happiness awoke my heart.
My darkest night was turned into day
When the violin began to play.

LIGHTING CUE 14

At the end of the song, the lights dim quickly to BLACK-OUT.
CRISTIANE *exits during the* BLACK-OUT.

SCENE 2

The Summer Palace Garden. The same evening

When the RUNNING TABS *open, the Garden is set for the* MURANIAN RHAPSODY BALLET. *The* CHORUS *and* DANCERS *in Gypsy and Tartar costumes are assembled. The principal characters are* A TARTAR CHIEF, A GEORGIAN GIRL, A GIPSY QUEEN, *and* AN ALBANIAN BRIDAL COUPLE. *The Ballet is in four parts and opens with the* DANCERS *only.*

BALLET*

MURANIAN RHAPSODY

Chorus *and* Dancers

PART 1
DANCE

PART 2
SONG AND DANCE

Chorus.
We bring a rhapsody to ring all night
Putting our cares to flight
Making the star-folk dance in wild delight.
Our rhapsody was born where ancient streams
Asleep, flow deep in dreams.

Mountain moon, look down
Where lovers wander hand in hand.
Misty mountain moon, look down
And bless our sleeping land.
Bow down and whisper to the alder shade
Your haunted serenade
That only love can understand.

PART 3
SONG AND DANCE

Awake my love, for Rapture sings
A tale of old enchanted art.
Awake, my darling, for my music brings
A message to your heart.

Proud children of the hills
Break off your frantic dance
For deep'ning twilight fills
Your meadows with romance.

Solo Voices.
Go, greet your love, her gentle heart is pining,
Go, meet your love, the mountain moon is shining.

Chorus.
Beyond the west the glimmer dies away,
The night has come for all too short a stay.
Oh, watch the east
Beware the break of day
For dreams that linger till the dawn, are shattered.

PART 4
SONG AND DANCE

Traitors, fear us. Come not near us.
Brothers, join us. Join our chorus.
Join our dazzling dance of triumph.

*See page 55.

SCENE 3

Swell our, swell our Mountain Song.
Swell our Mountain Song
Swell our Mountain Song
Swell our Mountain Song.

At the end of the Ballet, the CHORUS *move down stage.*

REPRISE

No. 27

"THE VIOLIN BEGAN TO PLAY"

CHORUS

SOLO TENOR. And then a violin began to play

The RUNNING TABS *close behind the Chorus*

SOLO BASS. Then all my doubts and fears were borne away.
SOLO TENOR. The music carried me to realms far above
Where I knew the meaning of love.
Safe in your arms at last
No more to part
Sweet tears of happiness awoke my heart.
My darkest night was turned into day
When the violin began to play.

She came here as a stranger
And as a stranger she thought to stay
SOLO BASS. No loving arms to greet her
No loyalty to meet her
BOTH. As she wandered on her way.
SOLO TENOR. Her homeland was calling
Her voices seemed to say:
SOLO SOPRANO. Come home, come home, come home
SOLO ALTO. But then a violin began to play.

CHORUS. And then a violin began to play
Then all my doubts and fears were borne away.
The music carried me to realms far above
Where I knew the meaning of love.
Safe in your arms at last,
No more to part
Sweet tears of happiness awoke my heart.
SOLO TENOR. My darkest night was turned into day
When the violin began to play.

LIGHTING CUE 15

At the end of the song, the lights dim quickly to BLACK-OUT.
The CHORUS *exit during the* BLACK-OUT.

SCENE 3

An Anteroom in the Palace

The scene is in front of a large tapestry front cloth with a door up R *leading to a corridor. There is an ornate writing-table* C *with a throne chair above it. Stools stand* R *and* L *of the table and there are two upright chairs, one* L, *and one* L *of the door.*

OPENING MUSIC   No. 28

When the RUNNING TABS *open, the stage is empty.* CRISTIANE *enters, crosses to the writing-table and rings the handbell on it. A* MAID *enters and crosses to* RC. *The music fades.*

MAID. You rang, Your Majesty?
CRISTIANE. There is no sign of Countess Vera?
MAID. Not yet, Madam.
CRISTIANE [*sitting on the stool* R *of the table*] She said she'd come straight to me. Marita, you are one of the people—you can tell me—you have a sweetheart?
MAID. Why yes, Ma'am.
CRISTIANE. Well, then—tell me, what does he think of the King's plan for the people?
MAID. The King's plan, Ma'am?
CRISTIANE [*rising and moving above the right end of the table*] Oh, you don't even know—then I shall tell you. For hundreds of years, you and your kind have been kept down—working for next to nothing —so that your Lords and their Ladies should live like Kings and Queens. Now the King hates that, and if he has his will today, all that will be changed. Wouldn't you like that?
MAID [*crossing to* R *of the table*] I don't know, Ma'am, some of our people try to make trouble and have meetings, but it never comes to anything. Besides, Ma'am, surely there'll always be the rich and the poor?
CRISTIANE. Yes, but not the very rich and the very poor.
MAID. You've always looked after the poor, Ma'am. They'd give their lives for you.
CRISTIANE [*crossing above the table to* L *of it*] But I don't want that—I want them to live their lives

VERA *enters and crosses to* C.

[*She crosses to* L *of Vera*] Well?

VERA *looks at the Maid.*

You may go, Marita, I'll ring when I want you.

The MAID *crosses and exits.*

Tell me quickly.
VERA. Defeated—an overwhelming majority.
CRISTIANE. The King . . .
VERA. He just bowed—almost smiled—as if he knew what the result would be—and dismissed the Assembly. [*She crosses to* RC] I had a carriage waiting at the side door—came straight here.
CRISTIANE [*sitting on the stool* R *of the table*] Oh, God—the selfishness—the ingratitude—and now what?
VERA [*crossing to* LC] He'll fight—you know he will.
CRISTIANE. If he has the heart. Vera, he's given years to this scheme—he's fought everything—the enmity of the nobles—even the apathy of the very people he wants to help. How can he fight any more?

ELENA *enters and crosses to* RC.

ELENA. You got here first, Countess. I looked for you. I could have brought you back with me. I had such a triumphant ride, hardly any stones and very few hisses. Cristiane, you look pale, you should have come. Nikki spoke very well, but of course it was a losing fight. How could he hope to wipe away a system that has lasted a thousand years with a ten-minute speech? [*She crosses and stands above the table*] Oh well, that's over, and we can go on in the same old bad way and vastly comfortable it will be, too. [*She sits in the King's chair*] Oh—this is like old times.
CRISTIANE. And what about the small courageous minority that voted for him and the Bill?
ELENA. Knowing this country fairly well—I should think they will be exterminated. One thing you've never understood, Cristiane—coming from your dear little democratic country, is that here there is not one King—every nobleman in Murania has a kingdom—which he rules absolutely.
CRISTIANE [*rising and facing Elena*] But—that's where it's all so wrong—it must be changed.
ELENA. Not in our lifetime, my dear—not in our lifetime.

SCENE 3   KING'S RHAPSODY

NIKKI *enters and crosses slowly to* RC. *He is deathly pale.* VERA *curtsies.* ELENA *rises and stands* L *of the table.* CRISTIANE *moves to Nikki and puts her arms around him.*

CRISTIANE.   Dearest, was it—very bad?
NIKKI.   Bad—yes, it was bad. I'm glad you weren't there, to see me defeated.
CRISTIANE.   No, never defeated.
NIKKI [*crossing and perching himself on the downstage edge of the table*]   Oh, by the way, Mother—thanks for the smile you gave when the result was made known. I shall remember that smile.
ELENA.   Well, it's time somebody smiled. Oh, Nikki, you used to be so gay—it doesn't suit you to be serious and high-minded. Very well, you've been defeated. After all, it's only politics—dreary things.
NIKKI.   It's not politics, it's the hearts and souls and bodies of a million people and their children and their children's children—it's the whole future. If this Bill had gone through I could have left Paul a heritage he could have been proud of, but what now, what now—what will he be, just another King in a land of Kings.

A FOOTMAN *enters.*

[*To the Footman*]   Yes?
FOOTMAN.   Your Majesty, the Prime Minister is here and begs an audience.
NIKKI [*rising*]   Vanescu, already! [*He moves above the table and sits in his chair*] Tell the Prime Minister that I will receive him.

The FOOTMAN *bows and exits.* VERA *moves as if to go.*

No, Vera, don't go. In fact, I'd like you all to stay and hear what I may have to say.

VERA *crosses to* R *of Cristiane.* ELENA *crosses to* L.

VANESCU *enters, crosses to* RC *and bows.*

[*He rises*]   Well, Mr Prime Minister, have you come to condole?
VANESCU.   No, sympathize, sir.
NIKKI [*indicating the stool* L *of the table*]   Then please be seated. I suggest we all sit. [*He resumes his seat*]

VANESCU *sits on the stool* L *of the table.* CRISTIANE *sits on the stool* R *of the table.* ELENA *sits on the chair* L *and* VERA *on the chair* RC.

I personally feel I've been beaten with rods. Now, Mr Prime Minister.
VANESCU.   Sir, a very grave situation has arisen.
NIKKI.   I quite agree with you. This country has just slid back five hundred years.
VANESCU.   When, sir, you were gracious enough to dismiss the Assembly, the Assembly refused to be dismissed—in fact, they are still sitting and are awaiting my return. They have sent me to—to . . . This is very painful to me, sir . . .
NIKKI.   I remember my headmaster used to say very much the same thing before he lifted the cane. You were saying?
VANESCU.   Sir, the Assembly demands your abdication.
NIKKI.   Demands!
VANESCU.   They have the means in their power to enforce your consent.
NIKKI.   Nothing can enforce my consent.
VANESCU.   Not even the safety of the Crown Prince?
CRISTIANE [*rising and crossing to* R *of Nikki*]   You would never dare!
VANESCU [*rising*]   Madam, a half an hour ago, a Squadron of Hussars left for Kalacz to take the Crown Prince into protective custody. What happens to him depends entirely on what His Majesty decides.
ELENA.   Vanescu, you have gone too far.

VANESCU *turns and faces Elena.*

NIKKI.   No, Mother, not far enough. Your Hussars will ride to Kalacz. I should like to see their faces when they get there, they will return empty-handed—the Crown Prince is already in protective custody, and has been for the past week.

ELENA *rises.*

His grandfather, King Peter, assures me that he is well and happy. So, Vanescu, if your Hussars need a long ride, let them ride to Norseland—it will take them three months. I think it is just as well that you should know that. Directly I decided to present this Bill I also decided that if the Bill were thrown out I would abdicate. My decision is unchanged—I abdicate freely—but on my own conditions.

VANESCU. Your Majesty is not in the position to make conditions.

NIKKI. On the contrary, I am in the most powerful position—the most popular figure in this country is in my hands, one threat to my little son and you and your Assembly would be torn to pieces. As a King I have failed. I've tried to put humanity into hearts that have no room for humanity. How could I succeed? I was a fool to think I could. But by the time my son attains his majority, you and your kind will be swept away. Doubtless you have some official document where I can sign my Kingdom away?

VANESCU takes a document from his pocket, opens it and puts it on the table in front of Nikki.

You have—already? I might have known—but let me see it. [*He studies the document*] Ah, I thought so. Her Majesty the Queen Elena to act as Regent—I shall delete that.

ELENA [*moving to* L *of the table*] Nikki!

NIKKI. I shall delete that—substitute my beloved wife—Queen Cristiane.

VANESCU. But, sir . . .

NIKKI. That is my one and only unalterable condition.

There is a pause, then VANESCU *picks up a pen and makes an alteration on the document.*

Kindly initial that.

VANESCU *initials the alteration.*

Thank you. And now all that remains is for me to sign.

CRISTIANE *turns and stands with her back to the audience.* VERA *moves to* RC. ELENA *turns and faces down* L.

I hope my hand is steady. I should hate posterity to say, "How drunk he must have been." [*He signs the document*] There!

VANESCU [*with a sigh of satisfaction*] We may publish this immediately? [*He picks up the document*]

NIKKI [*rising*] In one hour from now.

CRISTIANE *sobs.*

When I'm across the frontier. I don't want any disturbances—people are so sentimental over abdications. And now, Mr Prime Minister—I don't want to keep you from giving your colleagues the good news.

VANESCU *crosses and exits.*

CRISTIANE [*turning*] Oh, Nikki, but why—why?

NIKKI. My dearest, don't you see—with me this country has no chance. I let them down once and they have never forgiven me, but with you they've nothing to forgive—only to love.

CRISTIANE. Oh, Nikki—I'm afraid, I'm afraid!

ELENA [*turning*] Of course she's afraid—it was an outrageous thing to do—the affront to me.

NIKKI. You'll get over it, Mama—you'll have an admirable life, free to come and go—they might even regard you as a martyr if you behave yourself.

ELENA. Of course, Cristiane can depend on me to help her in any way I can.

NIKKI. That's one thing I'm afraid of.

ELENA. If you're going to be insulting I shall go to my apartments. I shall expect you to come and say good-bye.

NIKKI. Dearest Mama, don't you remember, we said good-bye twenty years ago.

ELENA *starts to curtsy and stops.*

ELENA. Well, that's one thing I needn't do any more.

ELENA *crosses and exits.*

NIKKI. Vera . . .

VERA *curtsies.*

SCENE 4   KING'S RHAPSODY

VERA. Yes—yes—I'm going.
NIKKI. But not before I tell you how deeply I appreciate your love and your loyalty.

CRISTIANE *sits on the stool* R *of the table.*

I shall know that she has one dear true friend.

VERA *commences to weep.*

[*He crosses to Vera*] Now, please, no tears.

VERA *curtsies.* NIKKI *raises her and kisses her on both cheeks.*
VERA *slowly exits.* CRISTIANE *bursts into tears.*

[*He moves to* R *of Cristiane*] No, dearest, this isn't good-bye, you'll come to me whenever you can get away—secretly, of course—that will make it more exciting. Dearest, I've so little time, I just want to talk to you for a minute about our son. I want him to be everything I am not. I have always thought of myself, he must never do that. I know he's only a little boy but he must be made to learn that he is here to serve and only you can teach him how. You see, a King—as I've discovered—a King has not only to be a King, he's got to be a father, a father to his people. And now—head up, fearless eyes, that's how I shall remember you, with love and deep, deep gratitude.

NIKKI *crosses and exits.*

REPRISE   No. 29

" SOME DAY MY HEART WILL AWAKE "

The RUNNING TABS *close*

SCENE 4

The Royal Box at the Paris Opera. Ten years later

The scene is in two parts. The front of the box, as seen by the audience *in the Opera House, is* L *and is furnished with two chairs. An archway leads from the box to the reception room* R, *which is furnished with two chairs and a small table with drinks on it. The stage is presumed to be down* L.

When the RUNNING TABS *open* NIKKI *and* MARTA *are watching the performance. The lights are dim.* NIKKI *is listless and bored, but* MARTA, *keeping up appearances, is bright and animated. She is using lorgnettes.*

The music fades, and applause is heard.

LIGHTING CUE 16

The lights come up.

NIKKI. He sings very well, that tenor. What's his name? [*He looks at his programme*] Enrico Caruso—he should do well. It's so long since I saw the great world amusing itself. How little they all change. Just deeper lines and thicker paint.
MARTA [*surveying the audience*] The Princess de Vailly is trying to catch your eye, do acknowledge her. Look, down there.
NIKKI. Disgusting old harpy! [*He bows charmingly*] All Paris seems to be here. Can't you hear them whispering, " So they're together again—how very amusing. What can they have to say to each other after all these years? "
MARTA. Well, they could say, " What can she be doing with a man who is madly in love with his wife and talks of nothing else? "
NIKKI. In fact, she's wasting her time.
MARTA. She doesn't think so.
NIKKI. And what does she think?
MARTA. She doesn't think—she remembers.
NIKKI. What do you remember, Marta?
MARTA. I remember a frightened, bewildered boy tapping on the window of my little room near the theatre in Bledz and asking me—me of all people—whether he should run away or stay.

NIKKI. And you said stay.
MARTA. And yet you ran away. It was always you who made the decisions.
NIKKI. What else do you remember?
MARTA. Wondering when you'd fall in love and what I should feel when you did.
NIKKI. And what did you feel?
MARTA. I think I behaved very well—sixty miles to Hervat in a closed carriage without a tear; but when I'd crossed the frontier, I cried for three days and three nights. I've never cried since—I don't suppose I ever shall—until . . .
NIKKI. Until?
MARTA. I fall out of love with you—then I shall never stop crying.
NIKKI. How can you love someone who's failed—so completely?
MARTA. You didn't fail, Nikki—you were just a bit before your time, and some day history will bear out what I say. I suppose you know that Vanescu has been keeping his eyes glued to this box? He's getting up—I think he's coming over.
NIKKI. How wise of Cristiane to get him out of the country by making him Ambassador. Clever girl!
MARTA. If he appears, do you want to be alone?
NIKKI. Good heavens, no! Our conversation will be purely social—what else could it be?
MARTA [*rising*] Then shall we go into the reception room? Besides, we were getting far too serious.

NIKKI *rises and escorts* MARTA *to the reception room* R.

This is supposed to be a gay, gala performance and it's a very deserving charity. By the way, what's it in aid of?
NIKKI. I haven't the faintest idea. All I know is that the sale of tickets went up with a rush directly my name was announced as Patron. I had no idea I was still news value. [*He pours two glasses of champagne and hands one to Marta*]
MARTA. You have become news value all over again. You should be gratified.
NIKKI. Yes, and why? Because in three days my small son will be crowned, and what, may I ask, is that to do with me?
MARTA. You know perfectly well that the whole of Europe wants to know your attitude to the Coronation. There are strong rumours that you intend to be there.
NIKKI. And take all the limelight away from Paul? Oh, no. Let the poor boy have his day of triumph.

VANESCU *enters* R. *He is now the Muranian Ambassador in Paris.*

VANESCU. May I intrude, sir?
NIKKI. No intrusion.
VANESCU. Madame Karillos. [*He bows and crosses to Nikki*]
NIKKI. Well, Your Excellency, are you enjoying the entertainment?
VANESCU. Excellent, a very well arranged programme. How well Calvé sang.
NIKKI. You should have heard Karillos in her prime.
VANESCU. Karillos? Oh, yes, Madame, you sang.
MARTA. Oh yes, I sang—in the dim ages.
NIKKI. Well, Your Excellency, what is your diplomatic mission tonight? I feel that you have one.
VANESCU. Purely a social call, sir.
NIKKI. Purely social. Some wine? [*He pours a glass of champagne for Vanescu*] The first for five years—I wonder why? [*He hands the drink to Vanescu*]
VANESCU. There have been rumours, sir—I know there could be no truth in them, but I wanted to be sure—that you are contemplating being present at our King's Coronation.
NIKKI. Ah, but not officially. I am a private citizen, you know.
VANESCU. The Muranians have never considered you as such.
NIKKI. Which Muranians? The Parliament or the People?
VANESCU. There are still some unruly factions left.
NIKKI. After ten years?
VANESCU. Your presence in the Capital could easily cause a disturbance.
NIKKI. I think you exaggerate. *If* I am there I shall be there as a proud father, even you must appreciate a father's feelings for his son on the greatest day of his life.

VANESCU. I have been instructed by Her Majesty's Government to take every step in my power to MUSIC
prevent your being there.
NIKKI. By Her Majesty's Government, but not by Her Majesty.
VANESCU. Queen Cristiane would not act in any way contrary to her Ministers' wishes.
NIKKI. That is where we disagree. The Queen uses her head, certainly, but where her heart is concerned . . . No, Your Excellency, allow me to know all about my wife's heart.
VANESCU. After ten years?
NIKKI. You are impertinent.
VANESCU [*putting his glass on the table*] On behalf of our Government I forbid you to go there.
NIKKI. Forbid? [*To Marta*] My dear, the interval seems to be coming to an end. [*He turns to Vanescu*] Will you excuse me?

>NIKKI *and* MARTA *put their glasses on the table, then* NIKKI *escorts* MARTA *into the box* L. *They sit and pick up their programmes.*

MARTA [*looking at her programme*] The last act of *Faust*—who have we? Melba—Plancon—Da Nesbe —it should be enjoyable—but what a silly story.

>VANESCU *gives Nikki a baleful look, bows to Marta and exits* R.

Nikki, why make an enemy when you have no intention of going—or have you?
NIKKI [*almost to himself*] He'll stand there by the High Altar, alone. No, not quite alone—she'll be there, but not too near. He's on his own now. The organ will murmur, the incense will rise, he might feel faint. He mustn't faint, he's a King. They'll hold the Crown over his head—it's too big and too heavy for him to wear. I found it too big and too heavy and I was a grown man, and he's only a little boy.

LIGHTING CUE 17

>*The lights dim.* MARTA *concentrates on the stage.*

>NIKKI *exits unobtrusively* L. *The music of the last act of "Faust" is heard off.* MARTA *turns to speak to Nikki and realizes he has gone. She puts her lorgnettes to her eyes to conceal her tears as*—

>*the* RUNNING TABS *close*

>*The music fades.*

SCENE 5

The Cathedral of Bledz, Murania

The altar and altar steps are L. *Across the back of the stage is a grille with gates* RC *and* LC. *Two throne chairs are set, one up* C *and one on the upstage end of the altar steps.*

When the RUNNING TABS *open, the ancient Coronation Ceremony of the little King is nearly over. The* BOY KING *stands on the altar steps facing* R, *with the* ARCHBISHOP *behind him, holding the crown over his head. Two* ASSISTANT ECCLESIASTICS *stand above and below the Archbishop.* CRISTIANE *is seated on the throne on the altar steps, with* VERA *standing* R *of her.* CRISTIANE *carries a bouquet of white roses.* ELENA *is seated on the throne up* C. *Gathered behind the left end of the grille are* LADIES-IN-WAITING, OFFICERS *and* COURTIERS. *Kneeling behind the right end of the grille are* PEASANTS *and* GIPSIES.

| THE CORONATION SCENE | No. 30 |

CRISTIANE, VERA *and* CHORUS

>CRISTIANE *and* ELENA *rise. The Hymn is sung in Greek.*

MEN.   O ev themonis petheon
ALL.   O pethalis ospe anthos enlimony
MEN.   Vasiliske vasilises tek na isin theou
ALL.   Kyrie eleison eleison
         Kyrie fil ase ton ikon
         Kyrie kratiste ke kaliste eleison

MEN.	God save the King!	MUSIC

The ARCHBISHOP *turns and places the crown on the altar. The* PEASANTS *and* GIPSIES *rise.* CRISTIANE *rises and sings an "Ave Maria".*

CRISTIANE. Mother of Heaven
Gaze on this child.
Watch over him and keep him
Safe and undefiled.
Fear and grief allaying
Near when his steps are straying
Near when his heart is praying.
Guard him when hopes are perishing
Guiding and softly cherishing
Ev—er more.

ALL. Mother of Heaven
Gaze on this child.
Watch over him and keep him
Safe and undefiled.
Fear and grief allaying
Near when his steps are straying
Near when his heart is praying.
Guard him when hopes are perishing
Guiding and softly cherishing
Ev—er more.

VERA *sings the Muranian National Anthem.*

VERA. Dear Land of song and liberty
We hymn thy ancient name.
Thy songs are strong and true to thee,
The champions of thy fame.
From age to age thy heritage
Shall proudly dwell secure.
On heath and hill thy spirit still,
Undaunted, shall endure.

CRISTIANE *approaches the Boy King, pays homage to him then stands aside.* ELENA *pays homage. A procession is formed led by the* ARCHBISHOP, *who crosses and exits* R. *He is followed by the* BOY KING, CRISTIANE, ELENA, VERA, *the* LADIES-IN-WAITING, OFFICERS *and* COURTIERS. *They exit* R.

The PEASANTS *and* GIPSIES *exit unobtrusively up* R *behind the grille.* CRISTIANE, *as she leaves, drops a rose on the altar steps.*

LIGHTING CUE 18

The lights dim as the candles are extinguished except for a wide spot focused on the altar steps.

NIKKI *comes out of the shadows up* L, *passes through the gates of the grille* LC, *sees the rose, picks it up and moves slowly to the altar. He kneels at the altar and prays for the safety of the young King.* CRISTIANE *is heard singing off.*

CRISTIANE. Some day my heart will awake,
Some day my heart will awake.
Ah!

CURTAIN

MURANIAN BALLET

The description given here of the ballet (page 46) is taken from the verbal passage that accompanies the music on HMV recording DLP 1010. It is reproduced by permission of the Gramophone Company and Mr Christopher Hassall.

" Torch-light at midnight, and a wooded gorge deep in Murania's heart. The folk of the wild are come with songs, dragging their mountain wagons, all bent to the work. They sling ropes or paint the earth, hoisting their painted tents to canopy where dancing fires rebound with flashes of zig-zag red and barbarous gold.

Then from the cyprus shade a shadow moves, weaving a winding measure : she is the bride—small wanderer from her far-off Georgian lands. Silent with joy, her slender body sings the wonder of love to the tune of a blown reed. And now her worshipper leans at her side, adoring, barely touching hands, dancing the ritual dance that consecrates his marriage in the hills.

Late-comers, guided by the kindled fires, crowd in from the chase, wearily shouldering the antler prize. Glad of the night, they drop their load and hug the brushwood blaze. But still the lovers, lost in their delight, swing to the climax of their ritual play.

Last to arrive, the Tartar Prince, clutching his small square battered shield, comes home with the pick of his men fresh from a border raid. Each claims his love—all but the chief. To him a girl swaying in pleated purple moves in beauty like the genius of the glen—lures him from thoughts of war to lead the dance.

The smell of dawn on the wind ! The feast at the height ! Wine has inspired the furies of love and battle, exalting the warriors' rage. And now the child of a neighbour tribe sees how the Prince is pleased, and frantic with jealousy—her dagger drawn—spins to his side. Her rival cowers. Caught by the wrist, at last she drops her blade and is rebuffed, overwhelmed by the passionate feasters (the dance of the crowd unconquered), the Lords of the Hills."

FURNITURE AND PROPERTY PLOT

ACT I
Scene 1

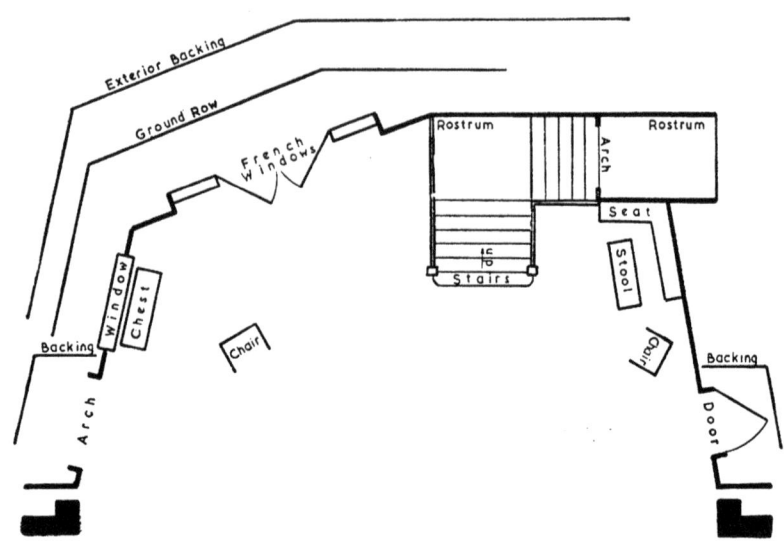

On stage—Chest. *In it :* scrap-book
   3 upright chairs
   Table. *On it :* Cake
   Long stool
   Armchair
   On walls : decorative plates, clock
   Carpet on stairs
   Carpet under low table L

   2 cushions
   Mattress cushions for built-in seats

Off stage—Necklace in case (PETER)
   Parcels, dolls, fir-tree boughs, bunches of flowers
   (CHORUS *and* DANCERS)

Personal—TRONTZEN : watch

SCENE 2

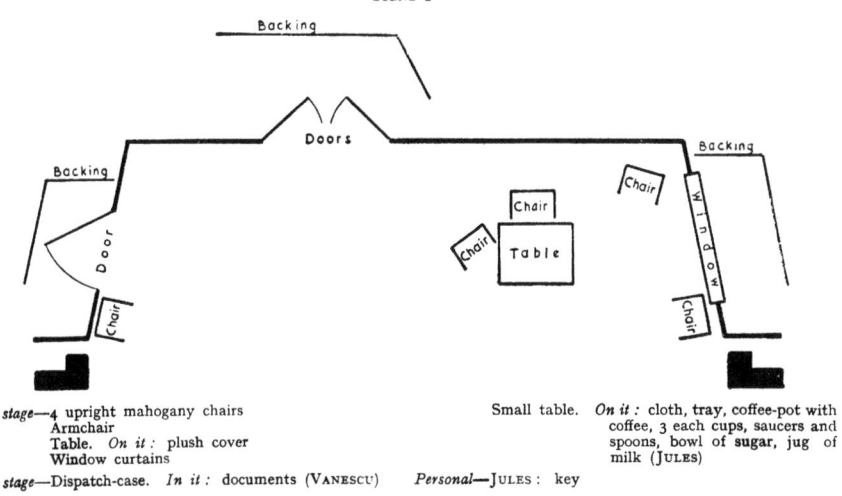

On stage—4 upright mahogany chairs
Armchair
Table. *On it :* plush cover
Window curtains

Off stage—Dispatch-case. *In it :* documents (VANESCU)

Small table. *On it :* cloth, tray, coffee-pot with coffee, 3 each cups, saucers and spoons, bowl of sugar, jug of milk (JULES)

Personal—JULES : key

SCENE 3

Front cloth only

Scene 4

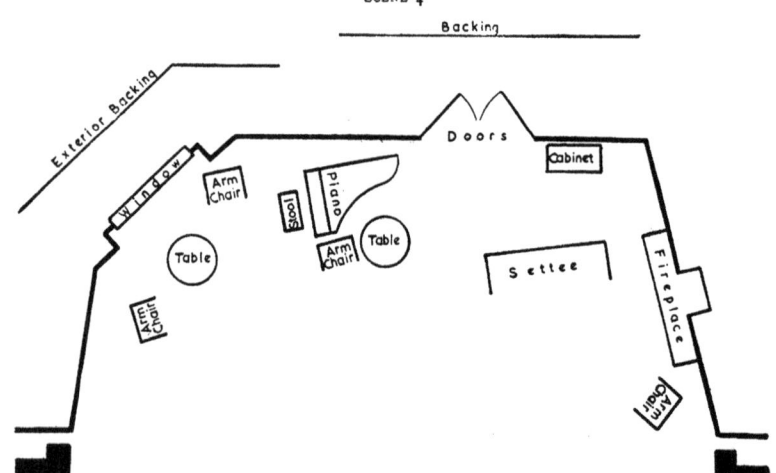

On stage—Ornate baby-grand piano. *On it:* bowl of white roses, bowl of flowers, manuscript music
Piano stool
Settee. *On it:* cushions
4 armchairs
Small circular table
Small oval table

Cabinet. *On it:* framed portrait
 In it: bottle of Tokay, 2 wine-glasses, corkscrew
On mantelpiece: clock, pair ornate branched candlesticks, with candles
Over mantelpiece: tall mirror
Fire screen
Window curtains
Carpet under settee

SCENE 5

Setting as Scene 4

SCENE 6

Exterior inset
Window with practical curtain

SCENE 7

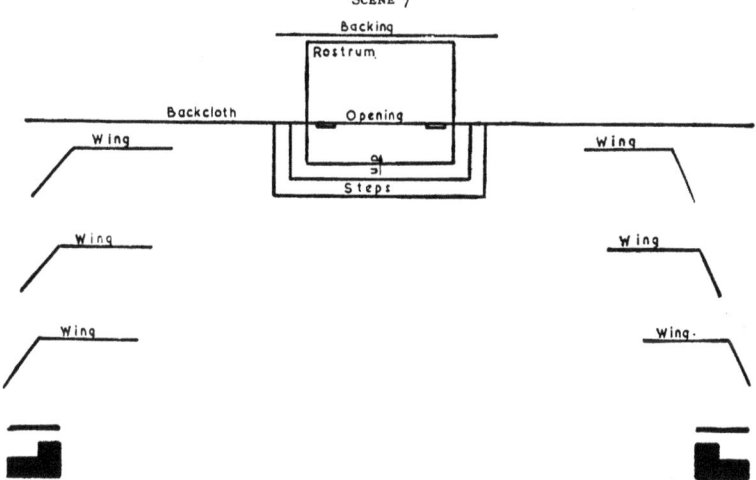

On stage—2 low tables

Act II

Scene 1

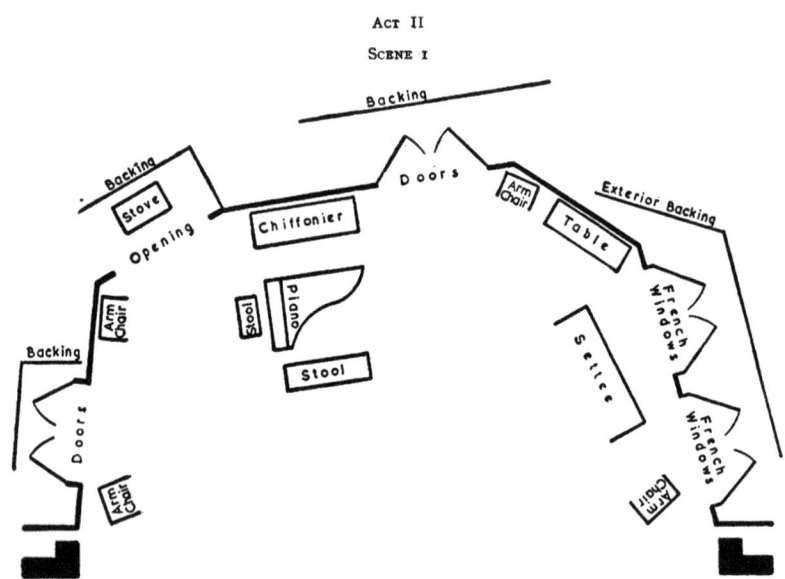

On stage—Long stool
Long settee. *On it:* cushions
Console table. *On it:* candelabra
Large mirror
Stove
4 armchairs. *On them:* cushions
Piano. *On it:* shawl as cover, manuscript music
Piano stool

Carpet
Window curtains
Picture on wall
3 sets candle wall-brackets
Chiffonier. *On it:* white cloth, bottles of champagne, plates of sandwiches, cakes and fruit, 4 trays with glasses of champagne.

Scene 2

Setting as previous scene

Strike—Buffet and glasses

ACT III

SCENE 1

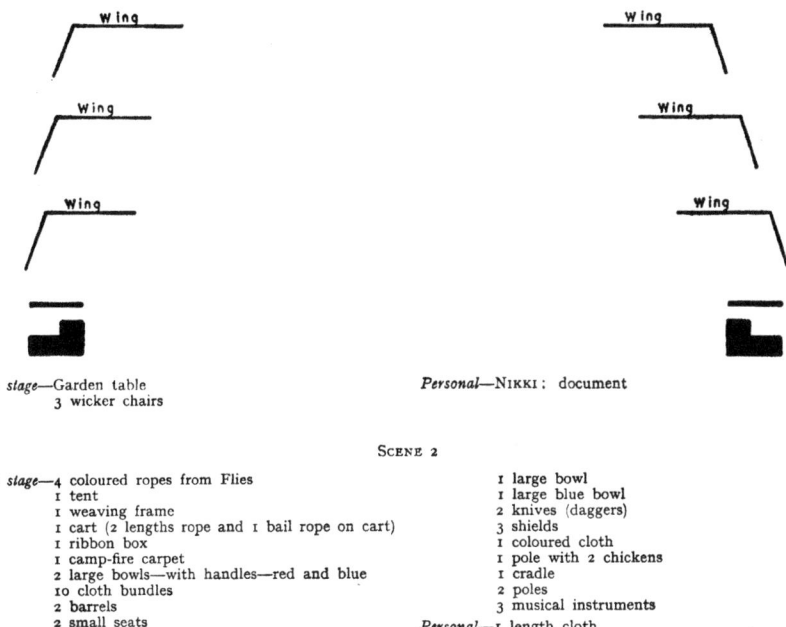

On stage—Garden table
  3 wicker chairs

Personal—NIKKI: document

SCENE 2

On stage—4 coloured ropes from Flies
  1 tent
  1 weaving frame
  1 cart (2 lengths rope and 1 bail rope on cart)
  1 ribbon box
  1 camp-fire carpet
  2 large bowls—with handles—red and blue
  10 cloth bundles
  2 barrels
  2 small seats
Off stage—4 shields
  4 logs of wood
  1 large bowl
  1 large blue bowl
  2 knives (daggers)
  3 shields
  1 coloured cloth
  1 pole with 2 chickens
  1 cradle
  2 poles
  3 musical instruments
Personal—1 length cloth
  1 wool winder

Scene 3

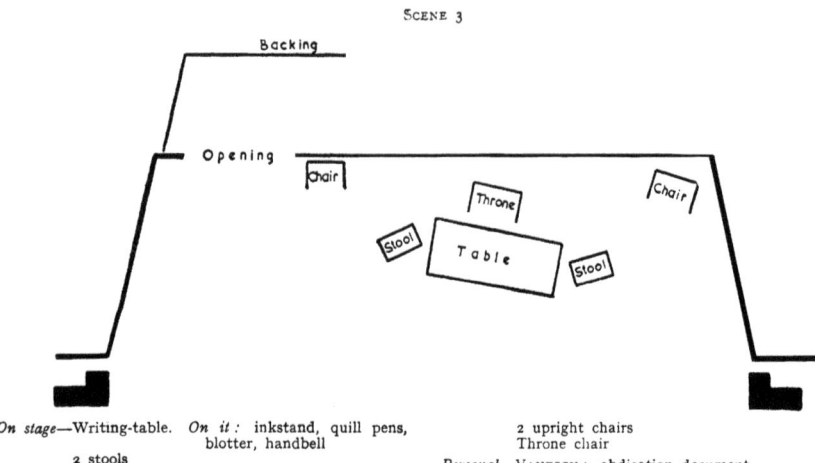

On stage—Writing-table. *On it:* inkstand, quill pens, blotter, handbell
2 stools

2 upright chairs
Throne chair
Personal—VANESCU: abdication document

Scene 4

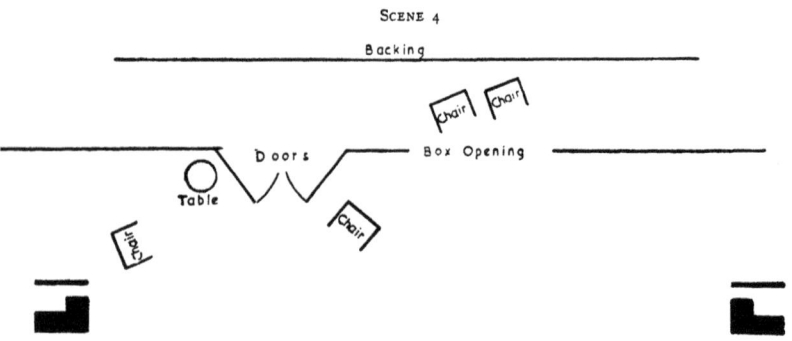

On stage—*In box:* 2 chairs
On box ledge: 2 programmes, small bunch of flowers
In reception room: upright chair, armchair table. *On it:* white cloth, silver tray, champagne bucket with bottle of champagne, 3 glasses

Personal—MARTA: lorgnettes

SCENE 5

Backcloth

Wing

Cut-cloth

Throne

Wing

Throne

Altar

Steps

Wing

Wing

On stage—2 throne chairs

Personal—ARCHBISHOP: crown
CRISTIANE: bouquet of white roses

LIGHTING PLOT

ACT I SCENE 1
Property fittings required—none
    Interior. Daytime
    THE APPARENT SOURCES OF LIGHT are large windows R and up RC
    THE MAIN ACTING AREAS cover the whole stage
To open: Effect of bright sunshine
Cue 1   At end of Scene   (page 8)
    Quick dim to BLACK-OUT

ACT I SCENE 2
Property fittings required—none
    Interior. Morning
    THE APPARENT SOURCE OF LIGHT is a window L
    THE MAIN ACTING AREA is C
To open: Daylight outside windows
    Dim lights on stage
Cue 2   JULES opens window curtains   (page 8)
    Bring up lights
Cue 3   At end of scene   (page 14)
    Quick dim to BLACK-OUT

ACT I SCENE 3
Property fittings required—none
    Exterior. Front cloth
    THE APPARENT SOURCE OF LIGHT is daylight
To open: Effect of bright sunshine
Cue 4   At end of Anthem   (page 14)
    Quick dim to BLACK-OUT

ACT I SCENE 4
Property fittings required—none
    Interior. Late afternoon
    THE APPARENT SOURCE OF LIGHT are french windows R
    THE MAIN ACTING AREAS are RC, C and LC
To open: Effect of late afternoon sunshine
Cue 5   During song " Fly Home Little Heart "   (page 17)
    Fade lights to BLACK-OUT *as* TABS *close*

ACT I SCENE 5
    Same setting as previous scene. Evening
To open: Effect of early evening light
Cue 6   CRISTIANE: . . . hearing the music   (page 22)
    Dim lights a little
Cue 7   CRISTIANE: Will she? I wonder   (page 23)
    Slow fade of lights to BLACK-OUT

ACT I SCENE 6
    Exterior Inset. Night
    A window C lit from behind
To open: Effect of moonlight
    Window light on

Cue 8   When window curtains close   (page 23)
    Switch off window light
Cue 9   As Serenaders exit   (page 23)
    Dim lights to BLACK-OUT

ACT I SCENE 7
Property fittings required—chandeliers (practical)
    Interior. Night
    THE APPARENT SOURCES OF LIGHT are pendant chandeliers
    THE MAIN ACTING AREAS are up C, C, RC and LC
To open: All lights full up
No cues

ACT II SCENE 1
Property fittings required—3 sets wall candle-brackets (practical)
    table candelabra
    Interior. Evening
    THE APPARENT SOURCES OF LIGHT are, at night, wall candle-brackets up C and R, and a candelabra up L. In daytime, large windows L
    THE MAIN ACTING AREAS are RC, C and LC
To open: Effect of brilliant candlelight
    Brackets lit
    Candelabra lit
    Blue outside windows
Cue 10   Song " The Mayor of Perpignan "   (page 30)
    Dim lights except for a spot focused on Marta
Cue 11   At end of song   (page 31)
    Bring lights up to opening setting

ACT II SCENE 2
    Setting as previous scene. Late afternoon
To open: Effect of afternoon sunshine
    Brackets out
    Candelabra out
No cues

ACT III SCENE 1
Property fittings required—none
    Exterior. Daytime.
    THE MAIN ACTING AREAS are RC, C and LC
To open: Effect of Spring sunshine
Cue 12   At end of opening song   (page 43)
    Quick dim of all lights to BLACK-OUT
Cue 13   NIKKI and ELENA enter   (page 43)
    Bring lights up to opening setting
Cue 14   At end of song No. 25 " The Violin Began To Play "   (page 45)
    All lights dim quickly to BLACK-OUT

ACT III SCENE 2
    Setting as previous scene
To open : Lighting as set for Ballet
Cue 15 At end of Ballet   (page 47)
    All lights dim quickly to BLACK-OUT

ACT III SCENE 3
    Property fittings required—none
        Interior front cloth
        There is no APPARENT SOURCE OF LIGHT
        THE MAIN ACTING AREA is C
To open : Footlights full up
No cues

ACT III SCENE 4
    Property fittings required—none
        Interior. Inset
        There is no APPARENT SOURCE OF LIGHT
        THE MAIN ACTING AREAS are RC and LC

To open : Dim lighting
Cue 16 As music fades and applause is heard (page 51)
    Bring up lights to give effect of house lights in Opera House auditorium
Cue 17 NIKKI : . . . only a little boy (page 53)
    Dim lights to opening setting

ACT III SCENE 5
    Property fittings required—candlesticks and candles (practical)
        Church Interior
        THE APPARENT SOURCES OF LIGHT are altar candles L and numerous candles up stage
        THE MAIN ACTING AREA is LC
To open : Effect of candlelight
Cue 18 As CHORUS exit (page 54)
    Dim all lights except for a wide focused spot on altar steps LC

www.ingramcontent.com/pod-product-compliance
Ingram Content Group UK Ltd.
Pitfield, Milton Keynes, MK11 3LW, UK
UKHW021846210426
5322IPUK00022B/502